Finding My Voice

LEANNE MITCHELL

Finding My Voice

BOOKS

1 3 5 7 9 10 8 6 4 2

Published in 2013 by BBC Books, an imprint of Ebury Publishing.
A Random House Group Company.

Jacket photography by Colin Bell © Woodlands Books Ltd, apart from back
cover © BBC. Plates: all photography © Leanne Mitchell apart from plate 8
(bottom), plate 9 (top and bottom right), plate 10 (top and bottom), plate 11
(top), plate 12 (top and bottom), plate 13 (top) © BBC; plate 13 (bottom left
and right) © Island Records; plate 14 (top) by Holly Child © WellChild;
plate 15 © Pacific Coast News; plate 16 by Simon Wisbey © Decca Records.

The Random House Group Limited Reg. No. 954009

Addresses for companies within the Random House Group can be found at
www.randomhouse.co.uk

A CIP catalogue record for this book is available from the British Library.

ISBN: 978 1 849 90486 5

The Random House Group Limited supports The Forest Stewardship
Council® (FSC®), the leading international forest certification organisation.
Our books carrying the FSC label are printed on FSC® certified paper. FSC
is the only forest certification scheme endorsed by the leading environmental
organisations, including Greenpeace. Our paper procurement policy can be
found at www.randomhouse.co.uk/environment

Commissioning editor: Lorna Russell
Project editor: Laura Higginson
Copyeditor: Lindsay Davies
Proofreader: Wendy Hollas
Production: Antony Heller

Typeset by Carrdesignstudio.com
Printed and bound in the UK by Clays

To buy books by your favourite authors and register for offers visit
www.randomhouse.co.uk

This book is dedicated to my Mum and Dad

Contents

Finding My Voice

Prologue

'And the winner is...'

'The votes have been counted and independently verified. Bo, Leanne, Tyler. One of you is our winner and we are about to find out who...'

The thud, thud, thud of my heart in my chest was now so loud it was almost drowning out both Holly Willoughby and the screams of the studio audience combined. Was this really happening? I closed my eyes for a second to try and compose myself, but all I could hear were two voices in my head – one was excitedly egging me on, shrieking, 'She's gonna say your name! She's gonna say your name!' The other was cackling away like some kind of demented cartoon character: 'You haven't got a chance! You're standing there with Tyler and Bo on either side of you, cool as ever, and you look like the completely odd one out who just gatecrashed the party. Let's face it – you're just a holiday camp singer!'

'The artist with the most viewer votes tonight and the winner of *The Voice* is...'

Surely this could not be happening? I never for a moment thought I'd get this far, honestly that's the truth, yet here I was within seconds of the opportunity of a lifetime and I wasn't sure what was scaring me the most, the thought of winning or the thought of not winning. What if she did say my name – how the hell was I going to react then? I felt completely frozen as I waited for Holly to finish her dramatic pause.

'...LEANNE!'

Was that in my head or did she actually just say that? My hand shot to my mouth. Time stood still for a split second and I felt as if I was falling down a tunnel in slow motion. My body went numb and I looked down to the floor to check I was still standing. Suddenly everyone was cheering, the audience had jumped to their feet and Bo and Tyler were hugging me excitedly and shouting, 'Oh my God! You've won!' I was going 'Oh my God! I've won?' as well but more to convince myself this was actually happening than anything else, because somehow my brain wasn't processing the information. Had I really won?

Everything went a bit floaty then. It was like being in a film and I felt as if this was all happening to someone else and not to me. I felt a hand, I think it was Bo's, smooth my hair away from my eyes, but at the same time I think I may have been having an out-of-body experience. It was as if I'd stepped away from myself and was watching from afar this happy, dazed and flummoxed girl, who can't believe she's just won the first ever series of the biggest singing competition the BBC had ever seen.

Next thing I knew Tom Jones came bounding up on stage and gave me a big reassuring hug. This was getting more surreal by the minute. Had I really won *The Voice*? Tom was beaming and Holly had a big grin on her face too, so the signs were good that I wasn't just having some kind of hallucination.

Holly was now asking me something but to be honest the words were barely registering. 'So, Leanne, if you can speak, what do you want to say?'

'Oh my God! Thank you!' was all I managed to garble. I think my first instinct was to burst into tears, but even that I couldn't do because I was just so numb. I must have been in shock because I didn't seem to be able to find any appropriate emotion or response. Well, nothing I could say on live TV anyway!

Shock doesn't even begin to cover it – dumbfounded would be more accurate. I think in situations like this there's an expectation that everyone will have the same reaction, you know, screaming, jumping up and down and crying. But some people just can't register it and work out what's happening that quickly – and I was now realising I was one of those people.

'Can you believe it?' asked Holly.

'Um, no...' I spluttered. OK, I seemed to have completely lost the power of speech.

'Well, it's true,' beamed Tom. 'And you deserve it. This gives me confidence that there is justice in this world!' And he punched the air with his fist, which made me laugh and gave me a moment to catch my breath.

Holly flashed me another dazzling smile. 'So, Leanne, after this, do you now believe in yourself?'

'Erm, I'm starting to, yeah...'

'Well, believe in yourself: you have just got a recording contract; you are our winner of *The Voice*. You are who we've been looking for. Ladies and gentlemen, our winner ... it's Leanne!'

There was so much I wanted to say at that point but I was in such a state of shock I'd lost the ability to express it. I wanted to thank everyone so much and tell them they had no idea how much this meant to me. I never thought it was even a possibility that I could win. I know I *can* sing because I have never done anything else in my life. But did I think I was good enough? I have always had that question in the back of my head, and the truth was, not in a million years!

But there was one point during the final where I thought, 'Oh my God, just look at what you're doing!' I was singing 'Run To You' and I looked over and spotted Jessie J with tears streaming down her face and I remember thinking,

'Am I actually having this effect on people with my singing?' That's what makes it all worth it when you connect with people and make them feel something. That's what it's all about for me.

Half of me was overwhelmed to have won the show and the other half was scared stiff because I knew that from that moment on I really did have to prove myself. I had to show what I could do and make certain I was a worthy winner. But through all the drama and dazzle and commotion that followed Holly's announcement, I had one question racing through my mind, the most terrifying and at the same time most exciting question of all.

'OK, so I have just won *The Voice*! What the hell happens now...?'

Chapter 1

Wish Upon a Star

I've always had this niggling fear at the back of my mind – what would I ever do if I lost my voice? I can be a bit of a worrier, but occasionally this fear actually grips hold of me. It's like a recurring anxiety dream. Who would I be if I couldn't sing any more? Singing is as much a part of me as the colour of my eyes, my name and who my parents are. It has shaped my life and I honestly can't imagine a world where I'm unable to make music because it's all I've ever done.

My first memory of working really hard at my singing is when I was around five or six years old and – to prove it – I've got some very dodgy home videos somewhere of me doing 'The Loco-Motion' with my friends! We huddled around my mum, Anita, begging her to film us doing the dance routine we'd vaguely worked out. We thought we were great, chuffing around the living room like little steam engines, with the occasional five-year-old wiggle thrown in, and with a lot of 'jump ups' and 'jump backs'. We definitely thought we had the knack! Actually, remind me to destroy those tapes when I find them again...

Back then almost every girl I knew wanted to be Kylie Minogue, with her bouncy bubble perm and that big Aussie grin. I think part of her attraction was also the presence of the equally perky and smiley Jason Donovan. My mates and I must have watched the 'Especially For You' video on a loop, each of us watching excitedly as Kylie and Jason searched for each other and then loving it every time they were finally reunited at the end. It was as if the end always came as a surprise to us, so engrossed were we in that cheesy Australian love story.

One of my first memories of going to a gig as a child is travelling to London with my nan to see Kylie in concert at Wembley. An uncle of mine worked at a coach trip company and there were some tickets going spare. All the way on the coach I sang her songs and chattered away about what Kylie would look like, what she'd be wearing, what she'd sing, and even how her hair would look. Well, when we got there it was a miracle I could see or hear her at all, we were sat that far back. She was literally the size of my fingernail! All I could see was this sea of people in front of me and then a dot in the distance that I really hoped was Kylie.

I didn't mind though; she still had a presence that filled the place and I truly believed this was the closest I'd ever get to someone as famous as Kylie, and that was enough for me. Little did I know that just over twenty years later I'd end up singing on the same TV show as her. How random is that? If you'd have told me that then, as I was peering out at her from the back of the Wembley crowd, I think I'd have just laughed and said you were winding me up.

All my life I've lived in Oulton Broad on the outskirts of Lowestoft, which is a small seaside town just down the east coast from Great Yarmouth. What can I tell you about where I come from? I guess back in the late eighties it wasn't the most exciting place in the world, but the people were down to earth and unafraid of a bit of hard graft, whether it was working at the docks or offshore on the oil rigs. Actually Lowestoft does have one big claim to fame – oh yes! The local area of Ness Point has the unique honour of being named...the most easterly point in the UK. Please contain your excitement!

I suppose Oulton Broad was just a quiet backwater, but I never wanted to live anywhere else and I still don't. You couldn't beat the summers there as a kid – we'd either be on the beach at Lowestoft, Mum and Dad overseeing proceedings as me and my older brother Daniel battled it out to build the biggest sandcastle, or we'd be buzzing down the Broads in our little motorboat, an ice lolly dripping down my arm as I hummed along to New Kids on the Block on my

Walkman. Then it'd be back to ours for a barbecue (if Dad could get it started) and *Blind Date* on the telly. I loved that seventies semi on Cambrian Crescent – my bedroom up at the back of the house looked over endless fields which I just thought was the best thing ever.

According to my mum I screamed for the first year of my life, right from the moment I was born at the Northgate Maternity Hospital in Great Yarmouth. Maybe even as a baby I was already getting my vocal cords in order? Mum says I was quite a cute child with long wavy blonde hair and somehow I always had tanned skin even in the middle of winter. And after the dubious honour of being crowned 'Miss Barbie' at Butlins Bognor Regis, she signed me up with a local modelling agency in Norwich.

I can remember that first taste of showbiz quite clearly. I was seven years old and Mum took me to a photographer's studio, where they had created a kitchen scene, and there was this tall model playing my pretend dad, all for an Eastern Electricity advertisement. The table was set up for breakfast with butter, jam and a plate of toast and he was sat there reading a paper. He had these reading glasses on and I was totally transfixed by the fact they didn't have any lenses in them. I couldn't quite get over the ridiculousness of that, and dissolved into fits of giggles every time he peered over at me through these fake glasses. I so wanted a quick nibble on the toast and spent the duration of the shoot staring at it longingly, but it was only there as set-dressing and would've probably tasted like cardboard. Looking back I'm surprised I ever got to work again as a model after that first effort!

But my picture did make it on to the cover of the Eastern Electricity brochure. Woo-hoo! It doesn't get much more glamorous than that. I got paid something like £35 and we framed the cheque because it was the first money I'd ever earned. There were a few more photo-shoots after that one, including some kids fashion pages for our local paper *The Eastern Daily Press* – one of which involved me being dressed as a sailor!

Another story that goes some way to highlight my lack of commitment to the wonderful world of modelling was the time when I was supposed to do a children's swimwear shoot. I couldn't actually swim at that point so I had intensive swimming lessons in preparation for the big day. However when the date was finalised it turned out the shoot was going to be on the same day I was supposed to be going to Dinosaurland with the school. Modelling a kid's swimming cozzie or going to Dinosaurland? Hmmm. There wasn't any contest really. I wanted to go on the school trip with my friends and see dinosaurs, and not be hanging around bored, being made to wear clothes that weren't mine. So I made my decision. Luckily Mum wasn't the pushy type and realised I didn't want to model any more. By now I just wanted to muck around with my school friends playing tag or 'What's the Time, Mr Wolf?'

It was around this time that I started to get seriously interested in music. This was mainly because Dad bought me and Daniel our own little £20 keyboards. Daniel was more interested in his karate than his keyboard, and soon lost interest, but I couldn't keep my hands off mine. I'd listen to TV theme tunes and try and copy them – one of my favourites was *EastEnders*. In the evenings, I'd perch next to Dad on the sofa as he taught me to play 'Chopsticks' on it.

Right from the word go, the patterns of music made sense to me. I could see the shapes, hear the rhythms and instinctively feel the chords. It soon became clear, not just to my parents, but somehow also to me, that I had a flair for it. I still wasn't singing properly though, but that all changed with the arrival of a karaoke machine, which my parents bought me for Christmas. It was only a basic cheapo one with a few songs on a cassette player, a tinny sound and a tiny mike. But frankly it was the most exciting thing I'd ever seen. I was immediately smitten and forever glued to it.

The two songs on the tape I sang over and over and over again were 'Sailing' by Rod Stewart, which I became slightly obsessed with, and 'Don't It Make My Brown Eyes Blue' by Crystal Gayle. The machine had a little plastic microphone and I'd just sit on my pastel-pink bedspread and sing my heart out to the posters of Kylie and New Kids on the Block that were carefully stuck to my walls. That's all I did for the next couple of years – sing in my bedroom. I never sang in front of other people. Not just because I was way too shy for that, but also because it never really occurred to me. Singing made me feel good, it was as simple as that. I wasn't doing it with an audience in mind, I was singing just for me.

I started writing songs when I was really young, about eight years old. The first one I ever wrote on my keyboard was called 'Wish Upon A Star'. It was a Christmas song and it went: 'Wish upon a star, sitting by a stream, over Jesus's barn, in a moonlight dream...' I had a very big imagination when I was little and I loved a good rhyme. My mum still takes the mickey now about my little Christmas ditty. She'll start singing the song at me when I'm least expecting it because she knows it'll make me cringe! I wrote another song called 'Broken Heart'. I doubt I'd ever really experienced a broken heart at that age – but I'd heard the words and liked the sound of them. I dread to think what the actual song was really about, maybe about having to miss your favourite TV show because of homework. Who knows? I'd just write and write constantly, from a really young age. Every single day I'd come home from school and I'd be in my room playing or singing or writing and that's just how I was. Again, I wasn't writing these songs with a view to anybody else but me hearing them.

I think I must get my musical side from my dad. He used to play the trumpet in a marching band when he was younger and you couldn't keep him off the stage at karaoke, however much he protested he didn't want to be up there. When I was a kid, he used to work offshore on the rigs for weeks at a time, but whenever he got back we'd put his name down to sing knowing he secretly loved being in front of everyone belting out a tune, even though he'd protest and pretend he hated it.

I'm not saying he's the world's best singer or anything but he's certainly not the worst either – he's got a really deep bass voice. So, back then, when he was home for a week or two, we'd head down to the local pub for Thursday karaoke night, with some friends and family, put his name down, and he'd be up there like a shot, crooning to 'Always On My Mind' or 'Daniel', which I think my brother (Daniel!) put him up for!

My Grandad Bert was another one who thought of himself as a bit of a singer. He was a proper Londoner and used to go around singing in pubs back in the day. He was known as a bit of a crooner, but I don't think he was actually working as a singer. It was more down to the drinking he'd indulged in previously, and then he'd get on the tables and start singing whether anyone wanted him to or not. Rumour has it there may have been the occasional scuffle as a result of a few too many Scotches, but to me he was just a real character with a twinkle in his eye and lots of humour and spirit.

A few years later I learnt to play the organ (not the coolest of instruments, I know) and I'd accompany Grandad Bert singing along to the Righteous Brothers' 'Unchained Melody'. That was a really happy time in my life and when he died in 2009 it hit all of us hard. He'd suffered with heart problems all his life – he'd endured six heart attacks, four heart bypasses and open-heart surgery – and eventually his body just couldn't take any more.

Christmas at Cambrian Crescent was always a laugh and more likely than not we'd have a houseful – aunties, uncles and of course Grandad Bert. Each year the family would make me drag my organ downstairs into the living room and I'd play songs from my Christmas book like 'Santa Claus Is Coming To Town' and 'Jingle Bells'. Everyone used to sing along. Some were half-tipsy and shouting at the tops of their voices, but moments like that made me realise just how lucky I was to be surrounded by such good people, who knew how to love life and enjoy themselves.

I know I've been really lucky that my parents are still together and that they always put me and my brother first. There's no way I'd be doing this now if it hadn't been for their support and encouragement. Even though I am forever doubting myself nowadays, when I was a child they tried to instil in me a sense of self-belief. I look back on my really happy childhood and think: 'Yeah, it was fun, we were just always laughing.'

Those Christmases were the only times I allowed myself to play in front of other people. And that was only because I was providing the background entertainment; it was others taking centre stage and it was all just a bit of fun. It sounds so geeky when I think about it now because I really was a total music nerd. Sitting in my room all alone, playing my organ, singing songs I'd written myself – it all sounds totally uncool, but it's who I was. I never understood the look-at-me, showing-off attitude of some kids my age – for me the music itself came first and the thought of me being the focus in any way made me shudder.

Mum and Dad told me afterwards they used to turn the TV down in the evenings and sit at the bottom of the stairs listening to me, because they knew that if I realised for just one moment they were listening in, I'd stop. Not because I was being naughty or stroppy, but because I couldn't quite handle the embarrassment. Back then I didn't think of myself as a performer in any way, I was simply messing around with music because it was something I enjoyed and it made me feel happy. Which is a great feeling for any young kid to have.

Mum has worked for years at a reservations call centre for holiday parks, which were the places we always used to go to for our holidays. When I was eight we went away to Devon for my mum's birthday, and this is where I first sang in public. Well, when I say sang in public, I mean, nearly sang in public!

I suddenly decided I wanted to enter some of the talent shows that the resort always ran. I can't remember what prompted my shock announcement; it was just a gut feeling, and I decided to go with it. My first attempt was a disco dance competition. God knows why because I certainly couldn't dance – disco or any other way – and needless to say I didn't win it.

Next was the main talent competition. This was the biggie! At first the best part was lining up with the other kids and making friends in the queue. We were all dead excited and there was a sense of anticipation and being in it together. I really enjoyed feeling a part of it all.

I was queuing with a new friend I'd made earlier in the week. I had it all planned – I was going to sing 'Sailing' (of course!) and I was word-perfect thanks to my trusty karaoke machine. I was telling my new holiday friend all about it as we got to the head of the queue. When it was our turn the guy taking down the names asked, 'Are you both singing together?' Suddenly my friend chirped up: 'Yes, we are!' I froze. What?! Needless to say, later that day I decided I didn't want to do it any more.

I don't think anyone was massively surprised I'd backed down. They'd only just got over the shock of me saying I'd wanted to enter the show in the first place. But it wasn't that at all. It wasn't nerves, stage fright or shyness. It was because I just didn't want to sing MY song with her. I didn't explain it to anyone, because no one really asked me. And I'm glad I didn't have to, because I probably couldn't have put those feelings into words at that age. I don't think I was being mean; I just didn't want to share the song I'd worked so hard to perfect. I'd spent hours honing 'Sailing' in my bedroom – did this girl even know the song properly? Instead of telling her that, and hurting her feelings, I walked away and chose not to do it.

So Dad said he'd enter instead and decided on Chuck Berry's 'Blueberry Hill'. My family were always up for a laugh and for a joke they entered him under the stage name of 'Noel Theodopolopoudos' and that has remained his comedy stage name ever since!

Unfortunately for my dad this wasn't karaoke and he didn't know the song lyrics. It was a talent show with a band, so he had to get the words. The only way he could do that (in those pre-iPhone days!) was for him and my Uncle Martin, who was on holiday with us at the time, to sit in the car that afternoon listening to the song. They drove around the car park for half the day while they kept rewinding the tape to get the lyrics, scribbling down the words as best they could.

Then he had to perform it that night. We've got it on video: the band are playing away and you can see him trying to hide the scrap of paper with the words on in his pocket while at the same time desperately trying to sneak a look at them. At one point he's practically pleading with the band to speed it up – they were playing it way too slow so he kept circling his arm at them to try and hurry them along! Oh God, that was hilarious; the memory of it can still reduce my whole family to tears of laughter.

That night, watching Dad give his brilliant performance, I recall feeling a pang of regret. He was up there, having the time of his life and giving everyone else a great laugh. I wished I'd been brave enough just to do the song, but also deep down, I knew I couldn't have shared the experience on stage with my friend and especially not if the song was 'Sailing'.

I don't know where this determination or stubbornness came from. It almost seems out of character as I hated being the centre of attention back then, and even now I'd much rather share the limelight with other people than have the pressure all on myself. But I also recognise there was a need at an early age to do it alone. It was as if, on some level, I already knew I wanted to be a solo singer. Even then I was taking this journey seriously and I didn't need anyone else tagging along with me just for fun.

I suppose I can see personality traits of both my parents in me. My mum and dad are total opposites. Dad will talk to anyone; if we're on holiday, he'll go to the bar and he'll sit there chatting to the barman for hours – probably showing off about his daughter who's a singer or his son who's the best plumber in all of East Anglia, knowing him. Whereas

I'm probably more like my mum because she'll stand back at first and take in what's going on before throwing herself into things. She may be quieter than Dad – that's not hard – but like my mum I know my own mind and if I think something's wrong I won't flinch from saying it. I'd like to think I have a sense of determination under this shy exterior. You know what they say ... it's always the quiet ones!

The next time I felt the urge to perform was two years later when I was ten. We were on a family holiday in Cornwall at the Mullion Holiday Park. There was a talent competition on and, once again, I surprised everyone by announcing I was going to enter. I think there were rumblings of 'I'll believe it when I see it' amongst the family members who remembered my previous non-attempt. But they were very supportive and encouraging. Again I had that gut feeling of 'I'm ready'. It had been three years now of practising in my bedroom, and I had an urge to sing in front of people. And not just any people. I was prepared to perform in front of strangers.

Sadly I had abandoned the notion of doing 'Sailing', which was no longer one of the only songs I knew. What puzzles me though is my final song choice of 'Send In The Clowns', which is by the American composer Stephen Sondheim. It's a sad song about a much older woman looking back at her unfulfilled life, her regrets and her mistakes. Hardly an apt choice for a timid ten-year-old with very little life experience!

I think I just chose it because I had the sheet music. At this point I had a bigger keyboard as well (which we'd bought from my Uncle Martin), so I was getting into playing a lot more and I'd buy sheet music of whatever songs I could get my hands on. So 'Send In The Clowns' it was!

I had a natural gift for music in the sense that I could sit and listen to a song and learn it really quickly. But on the other hand I certainly didn't have much of a voice back then. It was so quiet and undeveloped it makes me laugh just thinking about it because it was completely the opposite to what it's like now. My voice has definitely grown with me.

On the day of the competition I was so nervous. This was totally stepping out of my comfort zone. As I made my way over to the park's club-house to practise with the band, my heart was thumping faster than it ever had before – but I was determined to make this big step. I knew it was important to see it through this time – not to back down, or change my mind, or mess up. I had something to prove, not necessarily to anyone else, but to myself. This was my test and I wanted to pass it.

I decided what I wanted to wear, which was this dodgy long burgundy skirt with buttons down the front and a little black body-top, accessorised with a velvet choker. Under it all I had these big black boots on. My mum called them my hobnail boots – they were chunky laced heels, which I thought were the height of nineties fashion and looked really cool. Mum sighed. 'Really, Leanne, are you going to wear that?'

'Erm, it's called fashion, Mum,' I replied in that typically sarcastic pre-teen way. I wasn't old enough to be wearing make-up or anything like that, but Mum did my hair up in a French plait and I thought I looked the bees' knees.

That night I walked up on stage and as the room went quiet, I could hear the blood soaring round my body. My heart was pounding, my hands went clammy and my chest tightened. But I'd done it – I was standing on stage. Then I glanced around the room and saw all the kids and families looking at me, expectant and hopeful. I gulped and scary thoughts started to engulf me. 'I could walk off right now … I don't have to sing … I could pretend to faint!' It felt so strange, almost surreal, and seemed to go on forever – but the music rescued me. As soon as I heard the opening chords I felt better. I tuned into the music and could breathe again. The thoughts drifted away and I found my voice. Admittedly it was a little voice that warbled into the microphone which was held in a vice-like grip between my two sweaty palms, but hey, I was singing and, for once, not in my own bedroom!

As the song played on, I started to relax more, but I can't say I actually enjoyed the experience. I was still like a rabbit in a burgundy skirt, caught in the headlights and frozen to the spot. I was too scared to move a muscle except for my eyes, which darted and flitted from one side of the room to the other.

I knew Mum was there somewhere and Dad was positioned at the side with the video camera on me. I kept thinking to myself, 'I'm not looking at them, I cannot look at them.' Dad was never without a video camera in his hand and I was always telling him, 'Put it away!' He'd have been filming me on *The Voice* if he could – but I did point out to him it was going to be on telly so he didn't need to bother!

Anyway, I think my rendition of 'Send In The Clowns' was not bad for a ten-year-old and I just about got away with it. It wasn't particularly good, as I couldn't really sing out at that point. I'd only ever sung to myself and in my room where I didn't need to have power or punch to my vocals. But I could carry a tune.

Somehow, to my utter surprise, I ended up winning the competition. It hadn't been about winning for me; it had been about having the nerve to go up there and sing, and about taking my love of music that one step further. I'd achieved that the minute I managed to finish my song, but I have to admit to have won that day was so exciting.

The look of pride etched on to my parents' faces and their enthusiasm when I won was a great feeling and I think helped seal my childhood belief that music, and now maybe even performing, was always going to be a big part of my life.

The prize was that you win a holiday to come back to the resort later in the year with all the other winners of the summer shows, for a grand finale at the end of the season. I thought that was so amazing – not only did my whole family get to come back to this brilliant caravan park in Cornwall, but also I was secretly thrilled at the thought I'd be performing again.

We went back a couple of months later but this time I wasn't so successful. First place went to a little girl, one of those precocious stage-school kids, who sang 'Jeepers Creepers' with a fixed grin on her face all the while she furiously tap-danced away in a red ladybird costume. You know the type, the ones who have probably been training for this moment since the day they were born. Second place went to two beaming pony-tailed girls in shiny leotards doing acrobatics, cartwheels and somersaults. And trailing in at a respectable third was me – refusing to move, refusing to make eye contact, wearing a long burgundy skirt with big bovver boots, and quietly asking the audience to send in the clowns.

I watched the jazz-hands winner thinking, 'Oh God, that kind of thing is everything I can't stand,' but at the same time I could see she was really good. I was fine with coming third because I thought to myself, 'I'm not the kind of kid that would do little jazz-hand dances and big fake smiles.' I knew standing still and singing the song was the way it had to be for me. Anyway, I didn't dare move in case I stumbled. I didn't have that childhood showbiz-type confidence. I think in an ideal world I would have asked if the whole audience could have shut their eyes while I sang. Or maybe they could've just left the room? That would have been the ideal scenario for me! Even though at that age I knew I was dreaming of being a singer, the reality of the situation was that I still wasn't sure if I liked everyone looking at me. So my ambitions were a really weird contradiction.

It was after this holiday that my parents suggested I try singing lessons, and it sounded like a good idea. Before that I'd had horse-riding lessons and at one point I'd had dancing lessons, although I wasn't ever any good at it. When I was four years old my parents had taken me to ballet and tap and for some reason I wanted to wear my tap shoes for ballet. They wouldn't let me, so I left. I'm guessing the whole dance path wasn't quite right for me...

I was already having keyboard lessons by then with a nice lady called Cathy Oldman at Allen's Music Centre, a music shop in Lowestoft. She was the one who'd first introduced me to playing the organ, which I'd picked up quite quickly, and through the next few years I sped through my grades.

Richard, my singing teacher, didn't believe in grades though. He said for singing you don't necessarily have to be a great singer to pass them, so I never took any. He used to train me more classically. I would do all my scales with him and he'd always have me sing pieces like 'Pie Jesu' and 'Ave Maria' and even 'I Feel Pretty' from *West Side Story*. I didn't like singing 'I Feel Pretty' at all – it wasn't a song I ever felt comfortable with. Too flouncy, girly and twittering, which wasn't me at all. But it was great practice for allowing the music to help me pretend to be someone else.

I also did a few singing festivals at St Andrew's Church in Gorleston. You'd have a judging panel that was made up of, well, music snobs, to be honest. They were so hoity toity and would snipe, 'No, that's wrong. You must sing it like this.' It would always be at eight o'clock in the morning on the coldest day of the year, so you'd be absolutely freezing and tired, and your voice wouldn't be warmed up either.

I wasn't in my element there and looking back, they did my confidence no good. When you used to sing, the judges had this piece of paper with boxes on and they had to mark one of the boxes. The boxes were labelled on a sliding scale from 'outstanding', 'very good' and 'good' to 'average' and 'poor'. I'd never get 'outstanding' or even 'good'; it was nearly always 'average' that they ticked. But it was the comments they jotted down on their bits of paper that would sting. They'd write things like 'She doesn't have to sing so loud!' or 'Too forceful!' At the time their criticisms hurt because I didn't know any other way to sing, but now I just think what they said is hilarious. I'm so glad I never let their ridiculous comments dictate my singing style or ruin my passion for music.

By now I was having my half-hour singing lesson once a week and I'd have my organ tuition once a week as well. When I was about eleven I started at a local club called Dusmagrik Young People's Theatre Company, which was run by Dusty Miller alongside her partner Margaret Miller. Dusty was a proper thespian and used to tell me off for how I was talking. If I said something like 'I'm goin' to a pa-eeh on Sa-err-day', she'd be aghast. 'You are going to a WHAT?' she'd boom. I'd reply nervously and correctly this time: 'I am going to a party on Saturday. Sorry, Dusty.' She'd make us all speak properly! I now appreciate the importance of diction when I'm singing, but at the time we'd give a big sigh and just want to be cool and talk like we were in *EastEnders*.

The first show I did was *The King and I* at the St George's Theatre in Great Yarmouth. We did a week's stint and I played one of the wives with a ridiculous big bun on my head and my own itchy home-made costume. You know at the end of the film when the king dies (sorry to spoil it for anyone that hasn't seen it!) and all the wives are there? Well, we'd all be actually crying real tears at the end of this thing. We'd got so into our parts, even at that age, it was as if he really had died. Even off-stage it would take us a while to compose ourselves – talk about dramatic!

I never got a big role. The main parts always went to the 'I demand you look at me!' jazz-hands brigade again, with their overbearing stage mums pushing their little stars forward. Whereas my mum didn't have a clue! Quite rightly she'd just drop me off and then pick me up afterwards. I'm sure she had better things to do with her time and I'm grateful for that. These things have to be gained under your own merit and steam, otherwise where's the pride if it's just your mum who pesters people into giving you things on a plate?

So because I was quieter I was always in the background playing one of the wives or a villager or a munchkin. Mum and Dad used to come and support me whatever I was doing in the shows, yet at the same time, knowing they were there always made me feel even more nervous. Still to this day I hate being able to see them when I'm performing, because then you feel like you're constantly looking over to see their reaction. Even now I'd rather not know where they are sitting in the audience.

In many ways Dusty was quite an inspirational woman and a lot of her advice has stayed in my head ever since. I used to get really nervous about going on stage and once she took me to one side and said, 'If you ever stop getting nervous then you shouldn't do it any more.' That was a light bulb moment for me and a relief to learn this is the way it should be. There is no shame in anxiety because nerves are adrenaline and that's what keeps you on your toes when you're on stage and helps you give your best performance. I still get like that now; I'm always on edge before I have to perform. I thought about Dusty a few times on *The Voice* when some of the other contestants said to me, 'Oh, I don't get nervous.' And I'd think: 'Well, what do you do it for then?'

Another time we did a music-hall type show and my song was 'She Sells Seashells'. Luckily for me I just had to stand there and sing it, but on the downside it was a total tongue twister! I sang it through once and then someone said to me, 'Get the audience to sing along with you.' And so the next time I sang it through once and then in the gap just before you have to repeat it again, I went 'Everybody!' and motioned for them to join me. But as I did it everyone laughed.

I remember thinking, 'What are they laughing for, what did I say?' I didn't realise that they were all going, 'Yeah, right, love.' I genuinely thought they'd all sing along once they'd been asked to; I hadn't meant to be funny. I did like the feeling of getting a laugh on stage though, albeit unintentionally. She shells sheshells – I still can't say it!

I always auditioned for the main roles but never got them. The very last musical I did at Dusmagrik was when I was fourteen and it was *My Fair Lady*. The girl playing Eliza Doolittle was off for one of the rehearsals because she had tonsillitis. They didn't have an understudy and so Dusty asked me if I would stand in and play the role in rehearsal, using the script. I don't know why, perhaps because at this point I was a bit older. So I did all 'the rain in Spain' stuff with both a cockney accent and then the posh accent and I totally enjoyed every minute of it.

Afterwards Dusty was really surprised. 'You are actually very good, Leanne!' she said. And a small part of me was thinking: 'But I've been here four years and I never got a decent role!' That said, I do realise this was also my fault because I never pushed for anything. It was all very well me not being aggressive in pursuing anything, but there is a point when you do have to work at things to make them happen. If you don't, you can guarantee there will always be someone ready to grab what you want just that bit quicker than you.

Even though her lovely partner Margaret had passed away only weeks before *The Voice* was due to air, Dusty still managed to find time to send me a card after my blind audition. 'Leanne, I have always admired your determination to keep going...' As I read I could feel the tears forming in my eyes. '...And now it seems to be paying off again. Even if you don't win, it's the taking part and being chosen that matters.' Yet again she'd nailed it on the head!

I was still singing in my higher voice most of the time and I didn't really get any kind of chest voice until I was about twelve, which coincidentally was around the same time I became obsessed with Whitney Houston and those big diva singers like her. As a result I was starting to find my singing lessons really boring because all Richard wanted me to sing was classical stuff and endless scales. He had other students with these lovely classical voices but I just wanted to sing like Whitney. At home, Mum would knock on my bedroom door to check I'd been practising my scales, but I'd be listening to Whitney or Mariah Carey, trying to sing like them because I wanted that kind of belting, pop voice. The funny thing is that now I really enjoy singing in a classical way and I'm so thankful that I had all that training. But when you're a kid you just want to be belting out the music that you love, don't you?

To be honest I never thought I really would be able sing like Whitney or Mariah because I didn't have the range they had to hit all those big high notes. So it was all a bit of a fantasy scenario for me at that point. Then one time I ended up being asked to sing 'Hero' at the Victoria Hotel in Lowestoft by a friend of the family and someone gave me a single red rose afterwards to say well done. I thought that was amazing. It made me think maybe I wasn't quite so incapable of reaching those big notes after all.

Barry Manilow was another singer I admired and I loved the way he wrote songs. I used to have this big book of his music and I would play his songs over and over again on my keyboard. The same goes for Michael Jackson. But it was the film *The Bodyguard* that first drew me to Whitney Houston. I was obsessed with that film, I loved all those songs and I'd sit there watching it thinking, 'Oh I wish it was me standing on that stage!' I loved the whole romance of her playing this fabulous pop star and Kevin Costner being there to protect her.

It's the fantasy and romance of it all, isn't it? It's that, it's her voice and it's those songs, especially the ballads, which I loved. I wanted to sing like that. I'd try and sing them and I still couldn't really hit all the high notes, but I just used to keep working, keep trying, determined to get there in the end. This is how I started to get my voice to work for me in the way I wanted. People seem to think I was born with this big loud voice, but I wasn't. I had to work for it.

I just loved Whitney's voice, and it was the same for Mariah Carey, Barbra Streisand and Celine Dion. My mum was also a fan, so between my collection and hers, I must have had all their stuff on CDs, tapes and old vinyl records. I used to listen to it all, every single song, without exception. The strength, the depth and the range these women displayed had me in awe. Not only did they have bite, they had beauty in their vocals. In 2007 Mum and I went to see Barbra Streisand in concert at the O2. We were right up in the gods because they were the only tickets we could afford. But I remember sitting there watching her and thinking: 'Wow, you're still brilliant!'

So even as a kid I was fascinated by what it would feel like to be that kind of singer. They were glamorous, strong and so confident. One of my favourite personalities was Shirley Bassey, and watching *An Audience with Shirley Bassey* on the telly one night I was blown away by everything about her. She must just hypnotise everybody who crosses her path. She'd inject so much emotion and energy into her performances, it was incredible. I remember watching transfixed as she cried at the end of one of her songs. To have that passion and be able to share it is a gift.

But really, if I was to be honest, at that point in my life it was all about Whitney, and that's why it's the craziest thing in the world that I ended up singing 'Run To You' on *The Voice*. I was fulfilling a life-long ambition; being able to sing that on TV was a very special moment for me. I was starting to become the singer I'd always dreamt about – but at the same time it was tinged with sadness.

It was while I was recording the early stages of *The Voice* that Whitney passed away at just forty-eight. I guess a lot of people may have unfortunately seen it coming, but as with so many other legendary singers we have lost so recently, it was still a shock and so so sad that the world had lost yet another tremendous talent. This was a woman who had influenced thousands of little girls like me. Whitney was someone special who had the magic to make us believe our secret hopes could one day come true. Weirdly, it was also a timely reminder for me that being a pop star isn't always like the glittery romance of *The Bodyguard*. For some people it can be a very lonely place. I guess if you don't have the security of trustworthy, loving people around you, things can get sad and dark and difficult.

But every time I sang that song on the show I thought of Whitney in her prime, all that optimism, hope, belief and power conveyed through her vocals. And I thought of me as that little girl absorbing and loving her energy and daring to dream one day I could sing one of her songs. I'm proud to have done that and I really hope she'd have approved.

Chapter 2

Lowestoft to London

My first paid gig was an experience I'll never forget. It was at the Beaconsfield Conservative Club in Lowestoft and I got a whole £20 to sing eight songs. To a thirteen-year-old that was big money! I thought this was the event of the year, but in reality I was just the support act for the main draw, The Rick Hallam Band, who were a popular country music group in our local area.

The gig was in the Conservative Club's function room and Dad had bought me this little PA system, so we got there early to set it up and have a sound check. I looked around the room so I could be prepared for the evening – there was a bar down one side, tables in the middle and a small dance floor in front of the stage. To be honest it felt enormous and I couldn't believe the place was going to be filled with people. To my young eyes this was big. I might as well have picked up the microphone and shouted: 'Hello Wembley!'

I was beyond nervous beforehand but wouldn't admit how anxious and apprehensive I was. My head was swimming with all the things that could go wrong but because I wouldn't voice my fears, they became manifested in grumpy behaviour instead. My poor mum was at the receiving end that day. She'd be asking about my outfit and I'd jump down her throat for no real reason. 'It's fine, Mum!' I would snap and stalk into the other room. Then the moaning started. 'My voice has gone. I don't think I can do it, nope, I definitely can't sing tonight...' But my patient mother ignored my melodramatics and let me get it out of my system. I suppose she knew when I finally got up there I'd be in my element.

That night I stood at the side of the makeshift stage gripped with nerves. This was it – this was really happening! I was being paid to sing to people like a real-life professional musician. Deep down the singer part of me was really excited, but the little girl in me was scared stiff.

I heard myself being introduced, I hesitated for a split second and then, with a sharp intake of breath, I stepped on to the stage and saw a sea of expectant faces staring back. A wave of dread washed over me. Then I took another look, and I saw all these people were smiling at me. I realised they were on my side and willing me to do well. Encouraged by this revelation, that knot in the pit of my stomach came undone and I felt slightly less intimidated. I was ready to start my professional singing career.

One of those things that has no hard and fast rules, is how to actually start a gig. Do you talk first or do you sing first? I didn't know and walked onstage still unsure about what to do. Dad was sat behind me manning the little sound desk, and as soon as I came on I said to him, 'Just play it...' He whispered back, 'Well, say something first!' Out of the corner of my mouth I hissed, 'No, just play the song...' He hissed back, 'Just quickly say hello...' In the end I almost shouted, but still through gritted teeth: 'DAD, JUST PLAY THE BLOODY SONG!'

At last the song's dramatic opening chord rang out. Right, I've started! Once that first number was under my belt, which was 'The Shoop Shoop Song', it was as if I'd climbed a mountain. Next was 'Close To You' by The Carpenters and then 'Get Here' by Oleta Adams. I decided to speak a bit. 'Hi, my name is Leanne and I'm gonna sing you some songs for the next half hour. I hope you like it.' And I think that was all I managed for the entire set.

For a long time I used to worry about what to say between songs. In the beginning I used to awkwardly mumble dull phrases like, 'And now I'm gonna sing you another song.' Or: 'This next song was once sung by Mariah Carey.' On it went in that brilliant vein. Not exactly the most riveting patter in the world – in fact it's a miracle the audience didn't nod off there and then. But as I got more experience I realised I just had to be myself and gradually got the knack of being able to let the conversation flow naturally between songs.

Despite the nerves I really enjoyed it. My set went down well and there were lots 'Aaahs', partly because I was so young. The atmosphere was great, there was plenty of clapping and it was a real thrill to my barely teenage self to see people having a good time and being entertained by something I was doing. Yep, I'd totally loved it!

My mum, who had now been joined by my ever-so-excited Auntie Netty, had sat at the back of the room and I realise now that she had been equally as terrified as me. Having supported me and dealt with my moods all day in the build-up to my first ever gig, she was so happy that I'd enjoyed it as much as I did.

A few years ago, I went back to that function room for a friend's wedding and was so looking forward to seeing this gigantic auditorium I had made my debut in. And it was tiny! I couldn't get over how small it was, and yet it had loomed so large at the time, and later in my memories.

By the time I was fourteen I had various regular pubs and hotels around Lowestoft and Great Yarmouth where I used to gig. Usually there would be a nice-sized audience, but sometimes there'd be three people and a dog, which meant it was a struggle to keep the flow going. Having said that, there were some occasions when there was literally no one in the room at all, and that really was very strange indeed.

One time at the King's Head in Kessingland I was booked to perform in the function room. I used to do three sets of forty-five minutes each, and by this point my set list had expanded a lot, so I could sing different styles to try and suit everyone. Anyway, as I was due to start there was only one man in the room, who had just walked in. He was a proper biker bloke, head to toe in leathers, with huge tattoos and a big bushy beard. He looked like a right hard nut as he stood there clasping on to his pint of beer. I looked at him out of the corner of my eye, thinking: 'Hmm, I don't think you're going to like my kind of stuff. Are you a Steps fan?'

As the night went on all his biker mates started turning up, all looking like full-on Hells Angels, so I thought the best thing I could do was to tell my very long joke about a rabbit and a cabbage (don't ask!). It's the only joke I've ever remembered and if I decided to tell it during a gig, it would usually take the whole night to finish it between songs. Only problem was, I was generally the only one who ever found it funny. Anyway, by some miracle on this occasion the joke worked and by the end of the night I had them all singing along to 'Doctor Jones' by Aqua! My mum still tells that story because she can't get her head around how I got all those scary bikers to join in with such a cheesy pop song

– and I'm not sure either. I'm just gutted that I didn't have 'Barbie Girl' to hand...

I performed quite a lot at the Lowestoft RNLI crew members' club – the guys there were brilliant people; they worked so hard but they were a great gang and always up for a laugh. When they had their annual Christmas parties or summer barbecues, I'd be their entertainment. As it was for the RNLI, I didn't ask for any money, which I was happy to do as it was one of my favourite gigs. But they'd still pass a glass tankard round at the end of the night for me, which was really sweet. I think I turned into their little mascot for a while.

One time it was their Christmas party and I'd bought a load of Santa hats and reindeer antlers for them to wear, as I'd decided that the last set would be a fun festive singalong. I'd also made a backing track and printed lyrics to 'Home From The Sea' as requested by one of the crew members. So everyone was up for it, except one guy who didn't want to wear the antlers. I mean, the cheek after I'd made all that effort! 'I ain't wearing them, I'm going home,' he insisted.

So as he made to leave I followed him out of the building and chased him up the street, and because I had a radio mike they could all hear me back at the gig pleading with this poor bloke to return. 'Come back, please don't be a party pooper!' I yelled. Maybe he realised he wouldn't win against a fourteen-year-old with a microphone and antlers, so he gave in and came back to a round of applause from a now very merry bunch. I'm pretty sure he enjoyed it in the end.

I was starting to get a name for myself around the area and people used to follow me from pub to pub to listen. Then fans would turn up with a picture of me, usually the posters from the windows of venues advertising when I was playing next. They'd carry in these posters and ask me to sign them, which I found a bit weird. I suppose that was my first taste of groupies and I have to admit to finding it all a little unnerving.

I was only just getting used to being the centre of attention whilst I was on stage and singing, but people knowing me off-stage felt strange. There was no reason at all to be paying any attention to me then. As I performed more my confidence in my act was growing but once I stepped off, and people were still looking at me, I didn't know how to react. I just found it all rather awkward.

I still feel like that in many ways so imagine how I reacted when I won *The Voice*! When I'm singing I feel so in control, but when I'm just being me and people still want to talk to me because they've seen me on TV, I don't quite know what to say to them, or what we should be talking about.

I'd been gigging happily for about a year when a frightening letter arrived, addressed to Mum and Dad. It was from the Education Authority and it said someone had sent them an anonymous letter tipping them off about me. They had been informed that I was doing these gigs and I shouldn't be allowed to because I was only fourteen years old and therefore underage. We were all gobsmacked by the letter. We had no idea we were doing anything wrong and hadn't even thought about my age or the legal side of things. It was just something that I did and that I loved doing.

I never found out exactly who sent the letter but I always suspected an adult who did the same kind of gigs as me. I don't know if it was down to jealousy or what, but it seemed ridiculous that a shy fourteen-year-old could make a grown adult feel so intimidated or threatened. There was plenty of room for all of us.

The stern letter stated I had to stop performing there and then, which was horrible to hear. There was plenty of confusion and frustration as I sat on the stairs listening to my dad phoning round cancelling gigs, but soon my frustration turned to anger and it dawned on me this couldn't be right. We had to find a way to fight it. Surely there was a way around this, so I could carry on singing?

I had thrived on being busy gigging and performing, but there had also been a small part of me that wanted to be a typical teenager with a normal routine life. There were times – not often, but occasionally – when I had wanted to have my friends round at the weekend for takeaways or go out to the local discos.

But as soon as I was told I couldn't do the gigs any more and I could therefore have that normal teenage life I'd sometimes yearned for, I suddenly knew I didn't want it after all. It was a light bulb moment for me. I realised, 'Hang on a minute, this is why I'm different. My music is a massive part of me and I don't want to be like a normal kid.' Finally it was obvious to me just how much I loved singing.

It was a huge relief when Dad found out we could apply for a licence from the local authority, which allowed me to work under certain strict rules. These included stiff regulations stipulating that I had to be accompanied by an adult at all times, that sort of thing. One of the rules, which made us laugh, stated that I must have my own dressing room. I was singing in pubs, for God's sake! The nearest I could get to my own dressing room was my own cubicle in the loos.

My dad was always there beside me, every step of the way. He sorted all my gigs; he was my roadie lugging my PA around; he'd be on the sound desk when I performed; and when I'd recorded a little demo covers album with me singing over backing tracks, he would send them out in a jiffy bag with an accompanying letter to all the different record labels.

We got replies from some of the record companies saying I was too young. I remember in those days if you got a letter back, even if it was a no, it was still a big deal, because it meant somebody had actually listened to your music. We got a few letters from some of the big companies like Virgin saying, 'She's too young but she is good. Contact us in a couple of years.' Even though it was a rejection of sorts, I was delighted.

Then I heard back from Global – a massive label who had some amazing people on their books – who asked me to go and meet them in London. I couldn't quite believe it because I'd got so used to all the rejections. Their offices were near Oxford Street in the West End. One of the reasons I remember it so strongly was because I really wanted to go to that big Topshop at Oxford Circus afterwards.

When we got in there, the place seemed so glamorous and busy. I just felt very small and very young. Dad and I were led into a big boardroom where some trendy men and women were seated and I was asked to sing. I was so nervous and I can't remember much of it, to be honest. It just went by in a flash and a blur. And suddenly it was over and we were back out on the street again.

Dad was really excited, and so was I to an extent, but not to the extent people might have expected me to be. I was sort of taking it in my stride, and not quite believing it. I'm still like that now – I don't like to get ahead of myself, and any excitement is always tinged with nerves and a panic about whether I'm good enough.

A few days later they offered me a deal and I remember

them faxing the paperwork through for my parents to sign on my behalf. It was a big contract and my family was thrilled for me. This was huge. This was life-changing. And that was exactly why I didn't want it.

I was scared. The reality of it terrified me. Suddenly I had people telling me I was going to be the next Billie Piper or LeAnn Rimes or Britney Spears, and that frightened the living daylights out of me. I was only fourteen, I didn't understand anything about the music industry, and I was happy with my life as it was. I went to school, hung out with my friends and earned my pennies gigging at the weekend. That was enough for me at that point. I didn't want or need this monumental change.

The whole idea of me having to go and have this new life in London was something I couldn't comprehend. I was too young, I couldn't have coped and I wasn't ready for it. So I said so: 'No thanks.'

Mum and Dad were stunned. They could barely believe I was saying no to this golden opportunity. They came into my bedroom to talk me round. Dad said, 'Why don't you want to do it? This is what you've always wanted to do.' But it wasn't, not really. Yes, I wanted to sing, but it wasn't my ambition to try and become a pop star. It was all too much, and I felt so bad telling them I wasn't going to do it. So Dad had to ring up the record company and explain that I'd turned it down.

It wasn't because I was immature, either. I was a working singer who'd gigged in clubs and pubs and was quite old for a fourteen-year-old. In fact I was wise enough to know that this was something I wouldn't have been able to cope with at that age.

Looking back it does sound mad, doesn't it? I think fourteen-year-olds these days are very different to fourteen-year-olds then. They are so much more savvy nowadays and if that opportunity had been offered to any young teenager now, they'd probably jump at it.

I guess some people would never understand why somebody would turn a recording contract down flat like that. But like I said it's just not what I wanted to do – it wasn't me, and I was happier singing around Lowestoft at weekends with my friendly pub folk. I was still young; I knew there was a whole big wide world out there, and one day maybe I'd be out there too. But that was just going to have to wait for a while – or at least that's what I thought.

A year later my dad found out about a local management company and record label who had a recording studio only about a twenty-five-minute car ride from our house. We decided it would be worth a chat with them so we arranged a meeting with the two guys who ran it at their studio. Their place wasn't anything special and it didn't seem as big and scary as the other record company I'd been to, and that was definitely one of the reasons why I liked it.

They seemed really enthusiastic about me and because it didn't involve moving to London, it seemed the perfect way for me to try and further my music career but stay local, meaning I could stay at my school and stay with my family.

So my parents paid for me to write and record an album in their studio and we signed a deal with them to promote the album because they had a record label as well. It was a very small independent kind of thing, and because we didn't know anything about the music industry and how things should be done, we put our trust in them. Little did we know the chaos we would later be letting ourselves in for...

By now I was fifteen and I really enjoyed making the album. This was going on all the way through my GCSEs and every day that I wasn't at school taking exams, or doing a gig, I was at the studio working on my music, writing, recording or singing.

I really enjoyed it because it was laid back and fun. I had been in a recording studio before, when I recorded some demos a couple of years earlier, but this was different. This time it was my own songs. When you write a song you have this idea in your head of what a 'full production' of it should sound like, and up until now I'd been trying to create this sound in my bedroom – on an electric organ! So to be able to go into a proper studio and create something from nothing was such an amazing experience. Especially at only fifteen. I was making my own album and every bit of it I enjoyed, from recording the keyboards myself to the backing harmonies and then finally the lead vocal.

Various musicians would come in and record their parts and then Richard, the sound engineer, would put it all together. Some of the songs I wrote were originally written as a ballad, but by the time they'd been played around with, recorded and produced, they would've been completely changed to an up-tempo pop song, in the style of artists at that time like Britney Spears and LeAnn Rimes. I found that so strange, but I loved hearing the immediate results and I although I still found it a lot harder singing in a studio as opposed to in front of an audience, I was really getting into it and starting to feel in my element.

Mum or Dad would drop me off in the morning and pick me up in the evening, and at lunchtime I'd pop into the town centre to the same little bakery and get my sandwich for lunch. So it was kind of just the way life was – it was sort of, 'OK, this is what I do now.' But when I look back and think how much I was doing in such a short space of time and at such a young age, it was crazy. I had my gigs, I was recording this album, I was at school still, I was doing my final exams and on top of all that, I'd also started singing at a local holiday resort.

Somehow, amongst all this, I was still trying to be a normal fifteen-year-old, have a boyfriend, have a social life with my friends and do what everybody else was doing.

Maybe unsurprisingly, around the same time, I started to become consistently unwell. I had glandular fever, became really badly anaemic and I was getting ill a lot of the time. God knows how I did it all as I was permanently run-down, but I just used to keep going.

I remember having this constant battle between wanting to sing and wanting to go and be with my boyfriend or go out with my friends. But I knew that if I wanted to become a professional singer, that would mean sacrificing that teenage time to a certain extent.

I went to the Benjamin Britten High School in Lowestoft and didn't tell anyone there about my singing apart from my closest and most trusted friends. I decided early on to keep those two elements of my life separate. I enjoyed school and was quite academic, but by the last couple of years I just wanted to get out of there. Not because I hated it, but because I knew what I wanted to do with my life and I was in effect already working to that end. I was on my path and school and exams weren't really going to influence or change that in any way.

I also could never understand why music lessons were so boring. You'd have to sit there and listen to a piece of classical music like Tchaikovsky or Vivaldi's *Four Seasons* and you'd have to write about the symbolism in the music or what you thought the themes meant. We were teenagers and even if we liked the music, it wasn't really speaking to us.

It was a bit depressing really. I didn't think you would get anybody into music by doing that kind of thing. I would go to one of the practice rooms with a piano in and I'd sit and play for the whole lesson on my own.

In my final year I couldn't wait to finish school so I could just do my music, and not have to worry about homework or exams any more. It was almost like it was getting in the way and slowing me down. It was also hard because I kept my music side out of school and never really talked about it. But the more dominant a force it was becoming in my world, the harder it was to keep the social side of my life separate.

I'd never talk to anyone about the fact that I was a working singer because I never wanted to make a big deal out of it, but at the same time that was hard as it was such a massive part of me. I don't know what it's like now, but when I was at school, high school anyway, you couldn't say stuff like that there. You'd be seen as showing off and I couldn't have tolerated anybody thinking I was a show-off because I was about as far from being a show-off as you can imagine. I was also smart enough to know that if you were ever perceived to be making yourself the centre of attention, or trying to stand out from the crowd, then it was more than likely you'd get bullied for it.

There was one time, however, that some of my friends and I decided to put on an out-of-school show. They were all equally into music and dancing so it seemed a natural thing to do. We kept it to ourselves at first and rehearsed during lunch breaks and after school until eventually we were ready. We used the ticket sales to raise money for a local charity called The Fightback Trust, which supported people living with HIV and AIDS. The show was a huge adrenaline rush and thankfully a great success.

It was after this show that it became apparent to my friends that I was a singer. I was also getting in the local papers a lot, especially on the 'What's On' page, where it would say things like 'Leanne's at the Red House Pub this week' or whatever, alongside a small picture of me. By now my management were generating even more gigs for me, including all sorts of fetes and events with the local radio stations like Beach and Broadland FM.

I was always travelling somewhere around East Anglia, here, there and everywhere, and my managers got this car for me. They called it a limo but it was actually one of those white Lincolns, and although it was really comfy once you were inside being driven about, I was mortified to be seen getting in or out of it. The interior was red velour, the windows were all blacked out and the whole thing looked like a pimpmobile – as if there was someone really famous inside instead of a fifteen-year-old schoolgirl from down the road. Classy eh?

They'd drive the limo up to some event or gig I was doing and I'd be sitting inside it while all these people would be coming around, peering into the windows trying to look in. I tried to be cool about it but it was so embarrassing. I'd be like, 'There's no one famous in here. It's only me. Go away, you'll be disappointed!'

Luckily as it was now exam season no one at school really picked up on any of this, which is just how much off their radar I must have been. I was friends with both the cool kids and the more academic kids so I never got caught in the gossip or the bullying, which just seemed to come from petty jealousies. I always had a head on my shoulders that was older than my years and if anyone tried to start any bitching – 'Oh, so and so said this about you' – I'd knock it on the head before it had even started so it never developed into anything.

I never actually got bullied directly – at least not in the physical sense – but I started to be spoken and bitched about behind my back. It was just small-minded jealousy from a few sad girls because stories about my gigging had started to emerge.

If they spotted I had a local gig coming up they'd say: 'Oh, we're gonna come to where you're singing at the pub and have a right good laugh!' But I'd just reply, 'Well, you can if you want, but I'll make sure they won't let you in!' It would be easy to become intimidated by them, and I probably was a bit, but I'd just put on a front and make myself think, 'Whatever you give me I'll give it back to you twice as hard.' That was the way I dealt with it.

One of my friends wasn't quite so lucky. We'd stayed behind late one day and this group of girls were all standing outside the school and for no reason started picking on her and calling her names as we tried to leave.

Suddenly one of them launched herself at her and started kicking my friend. She was crouched on the floor as this girl kept on and on. It was horrible, my friend was sobbing and they were just laughing at her like it was all a fun game. I tried to get them to stop but there were at least ten of them and I felt helpless because there was nothing I could do.

But then my mum pulled up in the car to pick us up, saw what was going on and stormed over. My mum is a titch but she drew up all five foot nothing of her and started going mental. 'What the hell do you think you are doing?' she yelled. Despite the hideousness of what had just happened, I thought it was hilarious how the bullies were all taller and bigger than her, yet they all ran off, terrified, as if she was the bloody police or something! Nowadays, we like to call her 'the Rottweiler'.

It was seeing situations like these that stopped me mouthing off about my singing at school. I didn't want to give them any ammunition or do anything that made those nasty cowards think I thought I was somehow special or better than them in any way. I knew I was no better than anybody else, I just knew I was different. My difference wasn't earth-shattering or front-page news, it was just that at the weekend I didn't have a paper round or work in a shop, but instead I sang in a pub. However I knew the bully wannabes might not see it like that, so best to say nothing at all.

During the time I was recording the album, I wrote a song called 'Party Of A Lifetime' in music class, which I recorded at the studio and later released in aid of the East Anglia Children's Hospice for children and young people with life-threatening illnesses. It had a cool cover with little white stick men on it and it looked really professional. It felt great having my first single and even better that the money was to go to such an amazing charity.

My management were setting up bookings for me all over the place, including holiday parks and clubs. We'd also sell the single there and people would ask me to sign it for them, which felt really weird. I was a nobody so couldn't really understand why anyone would want my autograph.

The next thing that happened was they wanted to do an official launch for the single at a venue called The Talk in Norwich. It was a show-bar type place, and they got the local press and TV's Anglia News to turn up. It was an event to highlight my charity single mainly, and to also be used to help promote my forthcoming debut album – even though in the end it was never actually properly released.

It felt like a real step forward. I was going to be singing on the TV news and seen by thousands of people. They brought in a stylist from Toni & Guy to do my hair and some professional dancers to back me for the single. There was a host to introduce us and the hospice brought along a couple of kids who were well enough and they'd made this beautiful banner with my name on it. One thing I remember clearly was that I had to sing 'Party Of A Lifetime' twice for 'TV purposes', whatever that meant. I mean, they'd filmed it, what did they need to film it again for? Later, when I appeared on *The Voice*, I realised this was something that happens all the time in TV land!

The children came on stage with me at the end of my set, which was quite emotional. They were so excited despite everything they were going through, and I was proud to be using music for somebody else's benefit. It still moves me that music isn't just something that can bring private pleasure, but it can also be used to help others in so many ways.

That was the first time I would ever be on the telly. We'd taped it for the six o'clock news so we rushed home to watch it. At the time of filming it the children had made the occasion so special that I hadn't felt too nervous, but now I was. How would I come across? Had I embarrassed myself on my first TV appearance? We were all crowded round the telly and I held my breath. When I appeared on the screen I felt a huge sense of relief at first because I looked OK.

But then I opened my mouth to speak – and oh my God! I couldn't believe what I was hearing. I sounded like a right bloody farmer. 'Allo, this 'ere is moy song, it is called "Paaarty

Of A Loyfetoyme".' I couldn't get over my Suffolk accent – it was awful. I mean, I knew I was a country bumpkin but this was ridiculous! Had I really been walking round all this time, talking like that? The shame! What gets me is, I was actually trying to do my posh voice when they interviewed me, so I had walked away at the time thinking I'd sounded pretty much like the Queen.

We did a lot of promotional gigs for that charity single, including several big corporate events. Then came the biggest show of them all. According to my managers, this was the opportunity to launch me, and the album, outside of the area where I lived. It was going to be big, and I was going to appear in central London. We were all very excited.

So where did my management choose to help catapult their sixteen-year-old protégé into the public eye? Stringfellows, that's where. Of all the places they could have picked, they chose a West End strip club.

Maybe at this point the combination of the red velour limo and the choice of club should have alerted me to the fact that perhaps my management team weren't quite as aware of my music style and, more importantly, my age as they should have been. Really, they just weren't right for me. But back where I came from, we didn't really know what Stringfellows was.

One of my managers had boasted he knew the owner, Peter Stringfellow, and he'd arranged for us to hire a private floor of the venue to hold the launch. Tickets went on sale through the local radio station, who put on coaches for anyone that wanted to follow me down to London for the gig – so that night Stringfellows was basically filled with people from Lowestoft.

So my friends, family and supporters took the coach, which would drop them off and then pick them all up again later on. Meanwhile, of course, I had to arrive in my pimpmobile, a.k.a. the red velour 'limo'. I knew which transport I'd rather have taken, and it wasn't the car!

The area designated for my showcase was basically a large, loud room, all black, shiny and glitzy. Because it was the middle of July, it was unbearably sweltering. The cost of the drinks were also bringing people out in a sweat, as we were so unused to London prices. My dad bought a round for just five people and it came to £50! They all stood there shaking their heads going: 'Flippin 'eck – it's not like that where we come from.'

Afterwards we were told by my management company that Peter Stringfellow himself had sectioned off a VIP area for us with free champagne but funnily enough we didn't know about that when we were there, and no one recalls seeing bottles of Bolly around the place. Whether that was true or not, who knows. Maybe it was just my management trying to big themselves up by making out they were best mates with the rich and the famous.

I sang six original tracks from my demo album, which seemed to go down well, but I probably shouldn't have been surprised given that most of them in there knew me and had travelled down especially.

It was only later that night when I walked through another floor that I saw a couple of scantily clad strippers writhing around a pole wearing next to nothing. I'd never seen anything like it in my life, and although I tried to be cool, I didn't know where to look.

I then made my way to the Ladies, and while I was in the queue, this woman turned around and asked if I'd had a boob job. I just stared at her in shock for a second and then explained that I was only sixteen and my boobs were all mine. I was mortified at the time because my mum was standing behind me!

This gig came back into my life after I did *The Voice*, when a newspaper excitedly ran a very big headline shouting 'Leanne's Strip Club Gig!' alongside a picture of me singing there. I know perfectly well who sold that picture and I guess they'd spotted the opportunity to make a quick buck, but I won't give them the satisfaction of naming them here. The story just made me laugh when I saw it in the paper – if that's the only supposed dirt they can find on me then I can't really complain, can I?

We left there in the early hours in our limo and by the time we got back to Lowestoft, I only managed a couple of hours' sleep. I had another gig later that morning. God knows whose bright idea it was to schedule that!

It did start to occur to me that maybe my managers and I weren't exactly on the same page. I couldn't work out if they knew what they were doing or not. But you know, I was young, they were supposedly the ones with all the experience and my parents and I had no one else to refer to as we didn't know anyone else in the music business. I have always been a person who gives someone the benefit of the doubt. I never believe the hype and I take all the talk of big things with a pinch of salt, but ultimately if you ask me to trust you, I will. But only once.

One of my managers said he had contacts in the USA and decided that we should try our luck out there. So that became the next big event and everything we did was about gearing up for this US trip, which had been penned in for December.

The pair of them were getting very excited about it but I was taking my usual step back from it all emotionally. I wasn't desperate to go to America, it wasn't my be all and end all, but at the same time I knew there was so much potential out there. There was talk of me writing a song for a film soundtrack, which was something I'd always dreamt of doing. America started to sound like too good an opportunity to miss and I wanted to believe it would all work out for me once I got there. But, needless to say, nothing went according to plan...

Chapter 3

Going Stateside

S oon the trip to launch me in the USA was all anyone was
talking about. My management team were constantly
bigging up some hotshot American manager who, having
heard my demos, had been impressed with my voice and my
songwriting and wanted to work with us Stateside.

My UK managers were now at fever pitch about the
trip, whereas in true Leanne style I was still trying to take
everything in my stride. There's always so much talk in this
business and, even though I was young, I was determined to
keep my feet firmly on the ground.

'It would be amazing if everything they're saying comes
true, but I'll believe it when I see it,' I told myself. It would
have been so easy to get sucked into their world and their
big talk, but it's just not like me to get swept away by it all.
Instead I listened to my own voice of reason. Not because I

didn't have dreams, but because by this point I was starting to wonder if my managers actually knew what they were talking about or whether they were just talking out of their backsides. I mean, how did two local guys from Suffolk have all these big contacts in the US, and were all these supposed contacts really going to deliver on everything that was seemingly being promised?

I didn't have a clue what was going on half the time and I wasn't 100 per cent sure that they did. They did seem to love the sound of their own voices, but I wasn't so keen so a lot of what they said went in one ear and out of the other.

The one part of the trip that really made me excited was that there was interest in using one of my songs on the soundtrack of a film that was being made. I can't remember what the film was called but I was told it was going to be about a singer, and one of the Goss brothers from eighties boy band Bros had apparently been signed up to play the lead in it.

Apparently they were keen to use my song 'Broken Heart' as the title track, the one I'd written years ago in my bedroom, that I'd later developed in the studio. If this happened it would be a dream-come-true moment for me. After being obsessed with film soundtracks like *The Bodyguard* for all those years, the thought of one of my songs appearing in another film about a singer would just be an incredible achievement.

At the time there was so much I wanted to get excited about. My management were talking about my ambitions becoming a reality – having my songs used for films, being involved in writing a film score, working with big producers in state-of-the-art studios. This was everything I had ever dreamed of.

I was starting to get excited but I could still hear this voice at the back of my head telling me to be careful. How much were my managers just talking the talk? Could they back up all the promises and what would actually happen when we got out there?

Looking back, it was obvious the voice at the back of my head was the only one talking any sense. In fact, the first cock-up happened long before we'd even got to America – it was before we'd even left Lowestoft!

Because I was sixteen, I was told I needed to have a chaperone so Mum agreed to come with me. She'd booked time off work and got a passport all sorted out – my parents hadn't been abroad for years before this happened. Then literally three days before we were due to go, I was called and told that Mum wasn't needed there. But when I spoke to the American manager, a man called Billy, he said: 'No, it's your management saying that she can't come.'

When I look back at my managers, I imagine that they were so strapped for cash, they just didn't want to have to pay for an extra flight and accommodation. The importance of my state of mind and my need to be chaperoned probably didn't even enter their heads. But they had excuses for everything and managed to talk me round.

The alarms bells should have been ringing louder than they were, but after talking it over with my parents we decided this was too good an opportunity to miss. They knew I was quite grown up for a sixteen-year-old, had my feet firmly on the ground and could be trusted to keep a level head.

The thought of travelling without either of my parents by my side was quite daunting, but I was the same as I always was and thought logically to myself, 'Oh well, I'll just get on with it. What's the worst that can happen?'

I'd never been to America before. I'd only ever been abroad once and that was to the Algarve in Portugal when I was eleven, but I now had to go on this ten-hour plane journey effectively on my own. I boarded the plane, brimming with excitement and anticipation. However two hours into the flight my managers were getting stuck into the drinks trolley and getting louder and louder and more and more annoying. It looked like they were treating this as nothing more than a holiday or a jolly. It wasn't that I didn't like them, it was just we didn't really have anything in common apart from work. There was no discussion of our itinerary or plans, so I quietly put on my headphones, turned up the volume and tried to block them out by watching a film.

I was taking loads of pictures from the plane as we came into San Francisco. I looked out of the window and took in the amazing landscape below. The buildings looked huge and my tummy started to flutter with butterflies. I was really here, this was really happening. But, by the time we'd collected our luggage and headed out of San Francisco airport, I was in a total daze. I didn't know it at the time, but it was the start of jetlag. I'd never experienced it before and the tiredness was overwhelming. All I wanted to do was lie down and go to sleep. However as soon as we got to the hotel, we had to dump our stuff and go out for dinner with Billy and his team.

Billy seemed like a genuinely nice guy. He seemed much more professional than my two numpties from Suffolk. But I was so drained by the jetlag, I just sat there picking at my food, barely able to listen and wishing my mum was there. At one point I nearly nodded off into my chicken salad.

The next day I had to get up at the crack of dawn to prepare for a big photo-shoot they had planned. I was whisked away to the hairdressers to have my hair cut and blow-dried. Then I had my make-up done, and it was a lot of make-up – more than I'd ever had on in my life. Then it was on to the shops where everyone was buying the clothes for me to wear. I had very little say, if any, on the outfits they were buying, and I don't think I was on the ball taking in what was being chosen, as I was still half asleep due to the time difference.

At the photographer's studio there were lots of people standing around watching me and I felt quite awkward as I attempted to strike a pose. Orders were being barked at me like, 'Leanne, look over here. Can you not smile so much? Can you smile more? Can you look a little to your left? Put your hands on your hips.' My make-up was being touched up all the time and my hair was being pulled at and teased up higher and higher.

I also felt increasingly uncomfortable about the things they were putting me in and as I slipped into the next outfit, I thought, 'I don't want to wear this.' They were trying to make me wear a grey jacket but with nothing on underneath and the zip undone further than I was comfortable with. All I could think was 'Urgh' and I kept pulling the zip back up, which they weren't happy about. I wasn't really showing anything, just skin, but it didn't feel right. To be honest, I didn't like what they were trying to make me do and it all felt a bit tacky.

The clothes weren't bad – in fact they'd got all this posh stuff and some quite famous labels. But the outfits were probably more suited to a thirty-year-old WAG than a sixteen-year-old who still hadn't grown into her body. I have no idea what image they were trying to give me – I doubt my managers did either. I mean, what did two middle-aged blokes know about styling a teenage girl?

'I don't want to wear this because you can see my boobs,' I said quietly but firmly about another rather skimpy top. 'Oh no, you won't on the camera,' someone replied brusquely, looking at me like I was the one being difficult. I wasn't reassured and I so wished my mum was there. I needed her to be there fighting my corner, holding my hand and telling me what looked right and what didn't. It felt like I didn't have any control and no one was looking out for me.

I've still got some of those pictures. I looked at them the other day and, I tell you what, in those photos I look a lot bloody older than sixteen. It was as if I was being done up like a much older adult. My hair was bouffed up to within an inch of its life, I'm literally coated in make-up and I look really uncomfortable in most of the pictures. My blank expressionless face is saying it all and you can tell I am loathing every minute of it.

When we finished shooting in the studio, we all trooped off to take some more photos in the city's Union Square and on the beach with the Golden Gate Bridge in the background, which was such a beautiful location. The views were unbelievable; it was just a shame I couldn't really look at them for long.

There was quite an entourage with us that day: there was the make-up lady and the hair lady (who were both with us all week), Billy the American manager, my two British managers, the photographer and another guy who was there as some kind of a minder. Quite why he was needed was never properly explained to me. But I soon realised it was probably better he was there…

As we left the studio, which was down a back alley, all of a sudden we heard this woman start screaming somewhere on the main street. It was a terrifying sound. Suddenly, out of nowhere this guy came hurtling past us, roughly pushing me to one side in his frantic efforts to get away. He'd obviously just mugged this woman for her handbag but at the time it was like my brain had frozen and I didn't realise what was going on.

I couldn't take in what was happening and didn't have time to think. Otherwise I would have stuck my leg out and tripped him up! All I could think was, 'Oh my God, I've never seen anything like this before!' The woman was still screaming her head off and meanwhile all these guys who were with me were just standing there, even the minder. Once I'd got over the initial shock and watched this man legging it away with her handbag, I shouted to my group, 'Why don't you go after him?'

But they all shook their heads. When I shrieked 'Why not?' they replied quite matter-of-factly that more likely than not he'd have a gun. 'A gun?' I gasped. This sort of thing just didn't happen where I came from.

At that point I thought, 'This is all horrible.' I actually hated it there. I was a long way from home and starting to truly despise every minute of it. Not only was I exhausted and unhappy, I could now add scared to the list. But we had work to do, so we all carried on traipsing round the various San Francisco locations. As the day dragged on, I was fading away as the jetlag continued to space me out. But on and on the shoot went. I was unbelievably knackered; it was probably the middle of the night again back home by now. I hadn't slept properly for at least forty-eight hours.

Again, when I look at those shots of me down on the beach, I can't help but wonder what image they were going for. I look so stupid – I know it was still the nineties but talk about extreme! There's one where I have this massive red fur coat on (which actually I kept and later gave to a local dance school), these red leather-look trousers, a red top, red sunglasses... I mean, what the hell? There was a lot of red! I look like some kid who's been rummaging through a dressing-up box.

Later on that day, just when I thought things couldn't get any worse, they did. We were in Chinatown and I clocked this scruffy weirdo guy shuffling up the road behind us. Was he following me? I kept turning around to check I wasn't imagining it, but every time I stopped, he stopped. He was definitely staring at me and I didn't like it. It was totally creeping me out. Maybe it was my age, maybe it was the jetlag, but my nerves were jangling, I was on edge and I was starting to get really fearful. Again I was very relieved to have the presence of the minder alongside us, which just a few hours before had seemed a completely unnecessary extravagance. Thankfully he engineered it so we managed to lose the freaky stalker.

As soon as we finished the shoot we hurried back to the hotel to change before dinner – which was the last thing I felt like doing. All I wanted to do was sleep. I really needed to get some rest and get my energy levels back to something resembling normal. So after dinner I was practically dreaming about the prospect of getting some much-needed sleep at last. By this time it was very late, but just when I'd returned to my room and started to relax, my managers turned up at my door. They were going to the bar for a drink and would I like to join them?

I told them no and shut the door, but after doing so I slumped on the bed and burst into tears. Couldn't they see how tired I was? Also even if I wanted to have a drink, had they forgotten I was sixteen and therefore not legally allowed? What were they thinking? It struck me I was effectively on my own in America, working there for the first time and not having a clue how to do it. Even something small like jetlag, I'd never experienced it before, let alone had to work through it. A little bit of advice and support from my managers would have gone a long way.

I may have had a sensible head on my shoulders but I wasn't worldly wise. I'd lived in Lowestoft all my life, surrounded by the security of family and friends. But in just one day, I'd worked with a group of total strangers who weren't interested in what I had to say, seen someone get mugged, heard talk of guns being everywhere in the city, and had someone follow me. That combined with lack of sleep meant I'd had enough already; I couldn't take much more. If this was what being a recording artist was like, then I didn't want it.

Instinctively I knew I needed to hear familiar and comforting voices, so I picked up the phone and rang my parents. It was the middle of the night back in the UK and Mum sounded bleary when she answered. As soon I heard her voice, it all came tumbling out. Between the gulps and sobs, I told her, 'I hate it here, I want to come home.' I was all over the place emotionally and they must have been worried sick. It was a mixture of tiredness, fear, a sense of being out of my depth and just the need to have someone to talk to.

My parents immediately rang my managers to ask them what the hell was going on. My managers had lots of reassuring words and agreed to take better care of me, which proved to be an empty promise.

The next day was another early start and there were more meetings and more photo opportunities with various photographers and journalists. Later on when one of these men (someone I had only just met) followed me back to my room, I didn't like it. He made me uncomfortable but I wasn't able to articulate that. At that age you automatically act polite to grown-ups. Really my management team should have been by my side at all times to make sure I wasn't put into these kinds of situations. But my managers were nowhere to be seen. My instinct told me not to let him know which room I was in as he stood there making awkward small talk with me, so I hovered by another door down the corridor until he went away.

For the first few days of that trip the feeling of loneliness and being on edge never left me. I had no one looking out for me, and was away from home for the first time in a stressful working environment. That is not a good feeling.

Another day I was with the make-up lady and the clothes stylist after we'd been working all morning, and we'd gone back to my room to grab a quick sandwich for lunch. I'd been up since 6 a.m. and it was the first break we'd had. I was knackered, and gratefully ate my sarnie as I took a five-minute breather. The ladies quickly retouched my hair and make-up, then we hurried back down to the hotel lobby. Waiting for us with a face like thunder was Billy, who proceeded to give the three of us a massive bollocking for holding everyone up. It was like we were naughty schoolchildren.

'That's it!' I thought and I got really angry, which is so unlike me. I know I was young, and maybe a little naïve in this new world, but there was no way I was letting anybody speak to me like that. I yelled at him, 'Who the hell do you think you're talking to? Don't you dare tell me how long I have to eat lunch! I don't work for you!' I would never normally speak to someone like that – I don't really like confrontation – but I was not about to let anyone think I could be treated like some kind of idiot. I was really furious, but at the same time I could feel tears forming in my eyes. Still, I got an apology and it never happened again.

Amid all the chaos in San Francisco, I have one totally great memory. My managers took me to this really fancy hotel with stunning views over the bay to meet a guy called Pete Escovedo, who played drums with Santana, and is a massive name on the San Fran music scene. His daughter is Sheila E who at one time was the drummer for Prince.

He talked to me about songwriting and suggested I play this big black grand piano in the lobby, and sing one of my songs for him. He seemed like a lovely man – it was all about the music for him and I could relate to that. It was great to spend time with someone who loved music as much as I did. Being in his company, hearing his stories, and absorbing his enthusiasm and passion for making music reminded me of the real purpose of this whole trip and why I'd agreed to it in the first place. It wasn't about hair and make-up or getting the right photos, it was about music. I knew I shouldn't ever lose sight of that.

The next day we had an eight-hour drive to Los Angeles and as we drove through the outskirts I thought, 'This doesn't look like the LA on the telly.' I was taken aback by how shoddy and scruffy it looked. All around us were boarded-up houses and run-down shops. Some parts looked deserted and others looked downright dangerous.

But then we drove onto Sunset Boulevard and I started to recognise this as a world you normally only see in films. I was getting over the jetlag by now and was starting to feel my energy and enthusiasm creeping back in again. I was ready to experience this city I'd heard so much about.

We stayed at the Bel Age Hotel, which was on another scale to anything I'd ever experienced. It was so grand and posh, shimmering with old-school Hollywood glamour. My room was a suite with two levels, featuring a huge separate lounge area. In the bathroom there was a telephone next to the loo and I remember thinking, 'Why would you need a telephone there?' I'd never seen that before.

The room had a balcony as well and one evening I was getting ready for yet another meeting and stopped for a moment to take in all the glittering lights from what must have been a star-studded première down the road. It was a 'pinch me, am I really here?' moment.

If I'd been there on holiday with my friends or family, I would've been having a whale of a time, but I was stuck with people I didn't know particularly well, and now even they had fallen out. Yes, my UK management team had clashed with Billy, my US manager, and I felt like I was stuck in the middle of this brewing row, which had led to a horrible atmosphere.

I don't know what had caused everything to blow up in everyone's faces like this, but I think it was because they all wanted to be the boss and none of them wanted to play second fiddle. Battle lines had been drawn and all they did was squabble like school children. I was the youngest one there but it felt like I was the only one acting even vaguely like a responsible adult. This was incredibly frustrating for me because unlike my Mickey-Mouse management team, it sounded like Billy clearly had some great contacts out in LA.

Billy had set up a meeting with a big Hollywood talent agency. They started talking to me about the film of *The Phantom of the Opera*, which they suggested I could possibly audition for when the time came, because they'd been so impressed by my vocal range. It seems absolutely mad now to think that these opportunities could have been heading in my direction, especially knowing how big that particular film was in the end. So there was all this very real, big, thrilling stuff being discussed, which should have been our focus, yet around me World War III had broken out.

My managers were so dumb that literally minutes before this meeting with the talent agency, they were arguing over which one of them should go in with me. In the end I just

snapped: 'None of you are coming in, I'm going on my own.'
It was like dealing with giant kids. I'm not saying I was an
angel or anything, but it really got that stupid at times.

They were like that at every moment of the day when a
decision had to be made. If we went to a restaurant they'd
argue over who I had to sit next to. Once we arrived at
The Ivy in Hollywood with some people from another talent
agency and, when we were shown to our table, they just
stood there bickering and refused to sit down.

'You're sitting between us,' instructed my UK managers,
then Billy barked, 'No, come sit next to me.' And all I could
think was, 'Really?!' In the end I just sat down and let them
decide who was going to sit next to me. I was embarrassed
by them but by that point I was almost finding it funny as
well. It was like being in a cartoon.

Putting this bickering aside, The Ivy seemed so special.
Everything about the place oozed pure class and A-list
glamour. Lucy Liu from *Ally McBeal* and *Charlie's Angels*
was sat on a table next to us, and over on the other side of
the room was Adam West, the guy who originally played
Batman on TV. I was looking around trying not to stare but
my brain just kept fizzing with excitement and disbelief. It
all seemed so surreal.

Even more frustratingly, my management team helped
me miss something I'd been really looking forward to more
than words can say. It was a meeting Billy had set up with a

close advisor of Quincy Jones, who is one of America's most influential record producers and the mastermind behind the careers of many of my idols, including Whitney Houston.

I'd grown up listening to the people Quincy Jones had worked with and I knew everything he'd done. To even be in the same room as one of his team was an honour. Anything this person would have to say to me would be pure gold. I knew that. Anyone with half a brain would have known that. Yet we missed the meeting. Can you believe it? The numpties were late and I missed out on one of the biggest opportunities of my life. And why were we late? Because they had got way-laid shopping for souvenirs and lost track of time. In retrospect they were a bit of a joke, but the joke was wearing pretty thin. Especially when it was making us look like a shambles and wrecking my chances.

One night, sitting in the hotel bar, the three of them had a meeting to talk about who was going to be my actual manager. I was there but no one thought to ask my opinion properly and it ended in another bickering session. It was so pathetic I just got up and left them to it. I don't think they even noticed.

Another time the pair of them turned up at my hotel room in the middle of the night, with dressing gowns on, waving around a bottle of champagne – or perhaps it was even vodka. They slurred: 'We're going up to the rooftop for a jacuzzi, do you want to come?' I was sixteen years old, for God's sake

– why were they asking me to have a jacuzzi in the middle of the night? I should have been shocked but at this point nothing they did surprised me any more. Maybe because I acted so grown up, they never really thought about the fact that despite all the bravado I was essentially still a kid.

Every evening I'd sneak back to my room and call Mum and Dad to let them know the latest goings-on at the madhouse. I always used the hotel phone to call them because I didn't have a mobile back then. Needless to say my managers were fuming at the end of the week when they saw the phone bill. Did I offer to pay it? Did I heck!

I also met a guy called Blair Underwood who's an actor and his brother Frank, a scriptwriter and director. Blair was in successful TV series like *LA Law* and films such as *Deep Impact*, and he and his brother were now producing a film called *My Soul to Keep*. After chatting about their work and my music, they showed me the promo of this film and asked if I'd be interested in writing a song that could potentially be used for the soundtrack. I was over the moon they were even considering me and offering me this incredible chance.

They were really nice guys, obviously proper hard-working people who were passionate about the project. Their conviction and commitment to their work really inspired me, so as soon as I got home I began working on a composition for them. I wrote a song, which I asked my management company to forward, but I never heard anything about it again. I put this down to my management team not following it up. They just seemed useless and lazy.

I do think that they were very irresponsible as well. Considering you have to be over twenty-one to drink in the States, they often seemed to forget I was sixteen. They took me to a club one night in LA, a proper club, and they were sat there with their vodka and champagne, and kept asking me if I wanted a drink. It's not like I'd never had a drink at that age, but I wouldn't drink over there. I said to them, 'Are you mad? I'm only sixteen.' But they laughingly dismissed my concerns and even said, 'Oh, you'll be fine because of who you are.' What does that even mean? It wouldn't have taken a genius to see the kind of guidance they were giving me was not exactly sound or appropriate advice.

Maybe it was a sign, but I spent most of the plane journey home throwing up because of some major turbulence. I was so sick. But once I got home, despite all the ups and downs of the trip, I did feel positive about what I'd achieved and learned whilst I was away. Taking away all the negative things that had happened, I'd met some great people and talked about some really cool projects; there was a massive sense of excitement and it felt like there were so many possibilities to follow up on. I was ready to knuckle down and get on with the work.

We started planning a follow-up trip for January and my managers kept banging on about a massive charity concert that was happening in New York. They claimed Billy wanted to launch me over there by getting me a spot in this concert.

Looking back, I'll never know how much of this really came from the American side, how much my UK managers cocked it up or how much of it was never actually true in the first place. Were they just feeding me crap to make me believe they were being proactive in my career?

Sometimes I wonder whether I was just being fed stuff to keep me busy. Another time they told me they'd spoken with Westlife's management – which I guess meant Louis Walsh – and could I write a song for the band? Songwriting was something I was really into and I was hugely excited about the idea of writing for other people. So I wrote a ballad called 'Anything', gave it to my managers and – surprise, surprise – I never heard anything back.

But I'd just do whatever they asked me because I still didn't know how much they were actually blagging. They were all talk and whenever I tried to get down to the truth, they'd always know how to chat their way out of it. They may have been amateurs about other things, but they were experts in the gift of the gab.

Also I probably continued to believe in them because I thought surely they would want this to be a success too. They must have known we could have gone places and made things happen with a bit of effort and hard work. When we first got back from America I remember them sat in Mum and Dad's living room telling them how amazing everything was, saying, 'This is really it now,' and telling my parents how we had to get back over there straight after Christmas. Who would want to mess that up?

I realise, looking back, one of them in particular was actually a decent guy, but he just didn't have a clue what he was doing in this field; he was totally out of his depth. The other one gave the impression that he knew everything about everything – his ego was out of control – but when it came down to it he was about as useful as a hole in a bucket.

Neither of them seemed to know what they were doing but they didn't want the guys in America to take over and said they wanted full control of the next trip. I was constantly getting emails from Billy saying, 'What's happening? We need to strike while the iron's hot.' It was so frustrating: here was the chance of a lifetime but my fate was in the hands of a pair who didn't seem to have my best interests at heart.

Soon January came and went and there was no sign of a trip to the USA materialising. I kept asking what the hold-up was but they'd be full of excuses as per usual. Then one of my managers called Dad asking for £10,000 to fund the return visit. My parents did not have anywhere near that kind of money lying around, so Dad said he'd try and get a loan. I was horrified and I told him immediately, 'No way, you are not doing that.' He insisted it was what he wanted to do, saying it was what I'd been working so hard for. But I absolutely put my foot down and refused to let him. I couldn't bear the thought of my parents getting into debt because of me.

There then followed much discussion about getting a local business to sponsor me to go over there. But I would have felt a huge responsibility for their money too, especially if it didn't come off. Again I said: 'No, I'm not having it. My management can get me over there. If this is big enough and they really think something's going to come of it then they'll get us there. If they aren't prepared to put any money into it I don't want anyone else losing theirs.'

I was still under contract to these guys, of course. I'm sure the contract would have been legally worthless, but the fact of the matter was I was still signed with them. In the meantime nobody knew what to do. Even though Billy kept calling and trying to get them to let me work with him directly, they didn't like the fact that he wanted to take over, so they were being stubborn and uncooperative.

I'm probably one of the most realistic people you'll ever meet and I refuse to get carried away most of the time, but even I could see that there were proper chances and real opportunities waiting for me in the States. Whether it was writing music or singing, I really felt something could happen there. But my so-called management team couldn't pull it all off and seemed to just screw it up for me.

Over the course of the next year everything began to fizzle out. The more I felt things slipping away, the more my confidence ebbed away too. I felt like we were flogging a dead horse, with my career and hopes being the dead horse. I'd put myself out there, faced my fears and given it my best shot, but I'd been let down and that hurt. I started to believe that this had been my one big chance in life, and I'd blown it.

One saving grace was I was back doing my regular gigs around Lowestoft, and I was loving it. Being on safe ground surrounded by people I cared about helped to keep me happy and kept my passion for music alive. I couldn't afford to go to America myself and I certainly wasn't going to let Mum and Dad or anyone try and find money for it, so that was that. But I could still enjoy performing locally and no one could take that from me.

When I turned eighteen I wrote a letter to my managers and told them I was terminating the contract. I just woke up one day and thought, 'Sod this. I'm not interested in that fake showbiz world, not if that's the way it's gonna be.' I hadn't been paid a penny the whole time I'd been with them. All the promotional concerts and gigs they'd arranged, everything I did – I never got paid for any of it. Whether they did or not, who knows? Annoyingly, despite me not seeing any payment the entire time, they even tried to get money out of me for ending my contract.

There was some other interest from record companies over the period that followed but that initial experience had made me very wary. So I tended to have a distrustful attitude towards anything that was offered to me, or wafted in my direction. There was no way, after all the disappointments of that first time, that I could put myself through the wringer so soon all over again.

By now I'd got a full-time job singing at a nearby holiday resort and I was enjoying it. This was my opportunity to do something I truly loved for a living. It was honest and straightforward and that meant a lot to me. Yes, of course a Stateside recording contract would have been lovely, but my life was in the here and now and I was determined to make the most of it.

Chapter 4

A New Beginning

The fall-out from that recording deal taught me some hard lessons. I certainly didn't trust anyone and I was beginning to doubt if I had any real future in the music business at all. To start believing again meant putting myself back out there and there was no way I was prepared to do that any time soon.

Security and safety were what I needed and that's what I found at Potters Leisure Resort, down the road in Hopton on Sea. What that place gave me was somewhere to regularly perform and learn about music, be part of a team and feel happy. Oh, and it was there I found my future husband!

The first time I saw one of the shows at Potters I was so impressed, not only by how professional it was but also because it looked like loads of fun. It was a *Saturday Night Fever* medley that was being performed and there seemed to be so many people on stage having a good time. You could feel the warmth and energy filtering out into the audience, who were having a whale of a time too. I was absolutely loving it, clapping along in my seat, and I wanted to get on stage and join them right there and then.

Up until that point I'd always worked on my own; it had never occurred to me you could still be so creative alongside other people. But watching them work as one made me think for the first time ever that maybe I could be part of a group. It can be lonely always being on your own coping with the lows, and also there is no one for you to share the highs with either. I began to realise it might be good to have like-minded souls to lean on and learn with.

I first auditioned for the Potters Theatre Company when I was fifteen. Well, I say auditioned, it was actually more of an invite to come and sing at their Sunday lunchtime show before that week's guests went home. Mark Brewer (who was the entertainment team manager at the time) introduced me and then, to my utter surprise, sat behind me on stage, doing his slapstick routine – which consisted of pulling faces and putting tissues in his ears while I belted out 'Whistle Down The Wind'.

At first I was glancing nervously behind me. 'What on earth is he up to?' I thought, utterly flummoxed. I'd never sang with anyone else really, let alone had someone doing some kind of comedy routine behind me. Then I wondered if he was trying to test me by distracting me, so I played along with him, pretending I was oblivious to his gags and belting out the last big note as if my life depended on it.

I must have done something right because they asked me to come back – and this time I was going to get paid. The rate was £20 a show, not megabucks, but I could have punched the air with joy. It was the seal of approval I needed right then and gave me a much-needed injection of self-belief.

At that point I was just a featured singer and I'd only do one song, but on the first night I was due to perform, which was a big charity concert at the resort, my glandular fever flared up again. Mum and Dad were panicking that if anyone found out they might sack me before I'd even started. But luckily that didn't happen. I just about got through the night, singing 'My Heart Will Go On' by Celine Dion. It was the first of many hundreds of times I would sing that song there after that first evening.

I went from doing the odd couple of shows a week in between school and my own regular gigs, to the point where I ended up performing there nearly every night. Soon they put me on a weekly wage and I loved the fact I had a full-time job in this incredibly professional place and was making my living out of music. It may not have been a million-pound record contract, but to a teenager like me it was a very big deal.

On *The Voice* I kept being referred to as a 'holiday camp singer', which did make me laugh but it was also very frustrating for me. I knew it wasn't being said in a derogatory way, but I bet every time it was mentioned people were visualising 'Hi-De-Hi, campers!', knobbly knees competitions and Peggy Ollerenshaw (a.k.a. Su Pollard) and her Yellowcoat ambitions. But if anyone took the time to find out they'd soon realise Potters is not like that ... well, most of it isn't. And I've never once called Bingo in my life!

Potters is a five-star holiday resort in Norfolk and at the very heart of the complex is the Atlas Theatre where the theatre company put on a variety of shows. The standard of the entertainment there was consistently high because all of us in the in-house theatre company took a massive pride in our work. I was really happy when I was asked to take over the vocal coaching and arranging as well as being one of the principal singers. I could now also use my creative side, which helped shape so much of my musical knowledge and I gained so much experience.

I was in my element, absorbed by the music and the complexities of staging it. Every time I was given a new show to work on, I'd spend hours and hours sitting at home surrounded by sheet music, with my keyboard and a CD player. For days on end I'd be writing all these arrangements – it was a bit like being a kid in my bedroom again learning

TV theme tunes on my Casio keyboard (but maybe on a slightly different level!). I loved it.

As time passed the shows got bigger and bigger and I'd get more and more creative and confident with my work. Instead of just splitting the vocals between the singers, I'd start making original arrangements and coming up with quite complicated harmonies. I'd write each harmony line out and then assign it to a singer. When we started rehearsals I'd be in with the singers teaching it to them, line by line, until we had it all together.

On stage I would sing in any style going, everything from rock to opera, musical theatre to soul. One night it would be Adele's ballad 'Rolling In The Deep', the next I'd sing the classical 'Pie Jesu' and then the rock version of Wicked's 'Defying Gravity' or 'We Will Rock You' by Queen.

I loved singing the rocky stuff and I'd constantly try and push myself to sing higher or try more complicated riffs. I've always set myself a personal challenge to try and better what I've done before, whether I'm on stage or whether I'm singing to myself in the attic at home. I mean, thinking back to when I was ten years old, singing 'Send In The Clowns', I certainly don't think I was born with a great voice. I had *a* voice, but one that I would have to work hard on to achieve what I wanted it to do.

All those classical singing lessons I'd moaned about started to pay off because I had these two different voices

– soprano and 'belt' – which as I've got older, I've learnt to weave together a little bit. If I hadn't gone to those classes I wouldn't be able to do that and if it wasn't for Potters Theatre Company, I'm not sure I would have been able to experiment and develop this ability.

I also learnt how to be a tutor to other singers and at times I'd worry about the arrangement not being right, or it not coming together with the other performers. During this period, I was learning something else about myself – I was a bit of a perfectionist. I wanted things to be exactly right and was prepared to work continuously until they were. And I expected the same of others.

I got a huge kick out of encouraging the singers to push themselves too. Seeing people achieve something they'd thought impossible was as much a buzz for me as it was for them. I'd been doing so much mentoring at Potters, when I started on *The Voice* if felt really weird at first to have their vocal coaches doing that for me. But I instantly loved being coached. It was great not having to work everything out myself and I enjoyed being told by a trusted source what I was doing right or wrong.

What was harder was keeping quiet when it came to advising the other contestants. I was so used to coaching others, my natural instinct was to want to try and help if they were discussing any vocal problems, regardless of the fact they were my 'competition'. If I heard one of them talking about what to do for a croaky voice, I had to keep reminding myself: 'Shut up, Leanne, you aren't at work now!'

Potters also gave me the chance to perform with so many talented and brilliant singers over the years, from whom I could watch and learn. One I'll always remember is Lee Mead – who later shot to fame playing Joseph after winning the BBC's *Any Dream Will Do*. He'd just started at the resort, fresh out of college, and I had to teach him 'Somebody To Love' by Queen. Every single time he sang it, he sang at full throttle, hitting the notes every time, and then after the last held note he would always curl his lip and shout 'Yeah!', which without fail made me giggle.

He was brilliant and always gave 100 per cent, whether it was just singing to me or to the whole theatre. His nickname was 'Random' because he had a scatty personality in many aspects of his life. Except for his singing. Anyone could see that when it came to singing, he was completely focused and really did work his arse off. I admire and respect anyone who is dedicated like that.

Professionally I was full of admiration for most of the people I worked with, but when it came to matters of the heart, it was one of the resort's waiters who had caught my eye. I think the first thing I noticed about Rob was his curtains-style hair, which sounds terrible now, but back then in the 1990s, this was the David Beckham look and very on-trend. It wasn't long before he joined the stage management crew and I was delighted when we ended up in the same crowd. We clicked straightaway and about six months later we became a couple, and have been together ever since.

We moved into one of the older and unused guest chalets with some work-mates, and then into a bungalow, which we shared with my best friend Melissa and her boyfriend Darren. After that Rob and I branched out on our own into an old caravan for six months, which wasn't especially romantic or a great place to live. In fact, frankly it should have been condemned!

It had mould and damp in the bedroom and I couldn't sleep in there because it kept making me so ill. Instead we used to go to sleep on the sofas in the living room or a blow-up bed on the floor. I feel like I should blame that manky caravan for nearly ruining my twenty-first birthday! I had the worst cold ever and Mel had arranged a night out in London at the Tiger Tiger nightclub. I was dosed up on just about every painkiller you can think of and dragged myself down to the Big Smoke. Between sneezes, a fever, the sweats and blowing my nose, I just about managed to enjoy myself!

In my early days at the resort there was a real team spirit and I felt a sense of belonging for the first time in my life. We were in each other's pockets 24/7 and we called it the Potters bubble. This was our little world where nothing existed outside of it. I loved the sense of safety and security that came with that. We all watched each other's backs and after my experiences of bad management, it felt such a relief not to be out there on my own.

The occasional downside of this was we were in our own little soap opera and there was always a drama going on somewhere. Because our cocoon created a lot of couples, someone or other would always be having a row or going through a crisis.

Looking back it was a near-perfect time. We were all in our late teens or early twenties so we had disposable incomes (not that we were on a lot of money or anything) and we could just enjoy this period living free from adult responsibilities.

There was also nearly always a party after the show. These get-togethers weren't about getting drunk, but about letting our hair down and relaxing after a hard day's work. Our parties weren't wild but they were imaginative! Once Mel and I dressed up as St Trinian's schoolgirls; another time we had a party that was totally pink – pink outfits, pink balloons, pink cake. And one of my favourite celebrations was when we all chipped in and hired a huge adult bouncy castle for Mel's birthday.

We played hard but we worked extremely hard too. We'd always have about five or six shows running at the same time, so in a week you'd probably do a different show every night. And these were big productions so you couldn't afford to put a foot wrong. My brain would be swirling with everything I had to remember ... lyrics, harmonies, choreography ... and just generally what the hell was happening next!

Because I was one of the main singers, as well as looking after all the other vocals, I had to stay focused. There were many times when we would be in full-on rehearsals for a new show, still performing the current shows at night, and I'd be in the thick of new harmonies as well, so it felt like my head was about to explode. There were nights when I would collapse into bed exhausted, but I thrived on it. I was young, happy, earning a living from music and I wouldn't have had it any other way.

I think one of the reasons Rob and I go so well together is that we are similar. We both have stuff that we're really passionate about. He loves taking on challenges and trying new things too. Now he's an archery instructor but he's also into wall-climbing, air rifles, go-karts – he's even a qualified sky-diver. He's a proper daredevil and I love how fearless he is about stuff like that.

I tried climbing 'the wall' once, but I only got about five feet up and froze. And instead of helping me, Rob just stood there pissing himself laughing. I mean, he was practically next to me as I wasn't particularly high so I guess I can see the funny side! Whilst I wouldn't be doing anything quite so reckless as throwing myself out of planes or wall-climbing ever again, I know what it's like to be exhilarated and inspired by something you love doing. He also understands me and helps support me, and I him, which is so important.

I was feeling settled and at ease with my life by this point, but my best mate Mel was obsessed with me trying out for *The X Factor*. She was always telling me how there were so many more opportunities out there for someone with a voice like mine and she'd apply for me online every year, but I just ignored her.

Some of my other friends started pestering me about it too, so in 2006, the year Leona Lewis won, I gave in and agreed to go to the audition. I didn't really want to do it – I wasn't ready to put myself out there again – but nobody really understood my reluctance. 'What harm can it do?' they insisted, so to put an end to the pestering once and for all, I agreed to give it a shot.

My parents drove me to the audition at the Wembley Conference Centre in London and Rob came along too. I wasn't particularly nervous or excited. I was just going through the motions to keep everyone else happy.

It wasn't a great sign that as soon as I got inside the building, it became apparent the air conditioning wasn't working, so I was drenched in sweat and stayed that way for the whole day. After various off-camera auditions with producers, I was eventually ushered into the room to sing in front of Simon Cowell, Sharon Osbourne and Louis Walsh. Paula Abdul was also there, as she'd come over from America to be a guest judge.

At this point, seeing these well-known faces from a show I had enjoyed watching so much sitting in front of me, the stakes were raised and those tummy butterflies made a sudden reappearance. Actually, I was completely petrified as I absorbed the enormity of the situation I was in.

The famous panel looked up at me as I made my way to the audition spot. 'Keep your head up. Look confident. Keep smiling,' I told myself. Outside I'd been drinking gallons of water to keep my voice lubricated because of the heat, but as soon as I opened my mouth to speak my throat felt constricted and my gums completely dry.

I sang Carole King's 'Natural Woman' and when I finished, there was what felt like a long pause while I waited for the judges' feedback. Simon surprised me immediately by commenting that he thought, from hearing my voice, I could probably sing in a Katherine Jenkins opera style as well. I was impressed because it meant he could hear the classical training in my voice, which in turn meant he knew what he was talking about after all. Paula thrilled me when she said I reminded her of Kelly Clarkson at her first *American Idol* audition. For me that was an amazing compliment, especially as she went on to be the winner. Sharon was lovely, and told me I needed to try and be a little bit more sassy when I'm performing, which was probably a fair observation.

They then gave me the famous 'Yeses' and told me I was through to the next round. As I was about to leave, Simon noted my lack of confidence and advised me it was something that needed to be worked on. He suggested, 'When you leave the room I want to hear you scream with confidence.' So buoyed by passing this crucial audition and taking on board what Simon had just said, I bounded out of the room and screamed at the top of my voice.

Immediately I cringed at what I had just done. I would never normally make such a spectacle of myself. The emotion and pressure of the audition, meeting the judges and hearing what they had to say finally got to me, and I burst into tears. The presenter Kate Thornton was outside waiting and she swooped in to hug me, and of course the TV cameras caught every excruciating and embarrassing minute.

As I tried to calm down and compose myself, a producer appeared at my side saying 'Be more excited!' He was telling me I needed to show more personality. What they were asking for wasn't my actual personality though . . . they wanted somebody else's personality. I was incredibly excited but I like to keep my emotions under control and that was the opposite of what they were asking of me.

Somehow he persuaded me to run to Rob, who was in the waiting area, to tell him the news. Thank God I had asked Mum and Dad to stay in the car, because I hadn't been able to bear the thought of them in there, knowing it would stress me out.

So in the end I agreed and went hurtling off towards Rob who looked up and was horrified to see me, Kate Thornton and a camera crew, all heading straight for him. I just remember his panicked face looking at my panicked face and he literally jumped off his seat and ran in the opposite direction!

For Boot Camp, they put all the contestants up the night before in a Travelodge near Winchester. We were due to be up at 6 a.m. the next day and I had to share with some girl I'd never met before, who spent the whole night yapping on her phone to her boyfriend with the TV on full blast. I tried to be polite until about 2 a.m. when I'd had enough and snapped, 'Can you turn the bloody telly off please and shut up?!' She was so shocked, she did it.

The filming took place at a grand manor house and for the first few hours we just had to sit and wait in an empty room while camera crews went around to chat to some of the contestants and film them. However, it became apparent they were only speaking to the chosen few. No one came near me!

We then had to head out into the grounds for more filming. I took some deep breaths, thought about Simon and Sharon's advice and told myself: 'Just try and be more outgoing. Don't be afraid of the camera. Put yourself out there and get yourself noticed.' Of course, me being me, I wanted to camouflage myself and hide in the background, but I was determined to make a go of this and be more visible.

But I took one look at the other contestants and I knew I couldn't do it. People were being very, very loud and one boy was doing backflips while another girl was doing cartwheels as they were being filmed. My heart sank. I'd never been a look-at-me person and if that's what you had to do to get on this programme then I knew I was on the wrong path. I knew I could sing, and I knew I could sing pretty well, but as far as *The X Factor* was concerned I failed on all other counts. I wasn't an outgoing 'character' and I didn't have a sob story either. I suspected I didn't stand a chance.

Mobile phones were strictly forbidden, but I managed to sneak mine in. I hid behind a tree while I called Rob. I just needed to speak to someone I could be myself with, and someone who understood me. The rest of the day consisted of more hanging around doing nothing and I was so bored I just wanted to go home. I knew the competition was over for me. Finally at around four in the afternoon I was called to sing again. I remember being relieved I had something to do and this time it was for Simon and Sinitta, as well as a load of producers. I belted out 'Natural Woman'; they looked at each other, giving nothing away, and made some notes.

I thought it had gone OK as a song, but I was pretty much beyond caring by this point. As I came out of the room one of the girls going in next turned to me and went: 'Oh my

God, was that you singing? I don't want to follow that!' I think there was a compliment in there somewhere!

We had to wait for everybody to finish and it was about eleven o'clock at night when the results were announced. It had been one of the longest days of my life and I was tired, fed up and knew in my heart this process hadn't been quite right for me.

When I finally learned I wasn't through to the next stage, I watched people around me fall to their knees sobbing as if their hearts would break, but I felt strangely detached. My first thought was: 'Well, all that was a waste of time, wasn't it?' I vowed I would not be putting myself through a reality TV process like this ever again – at least that's what I told myself then!

I don't want to sound like I'm slagging off *The X Factor* because I'm not. I've always watched it and like so many millions of people, enjoyed it and got into it. There have been some amazing artists who have come from it. Also auditioning hadn't been a bad experience on the whole, and it had been really interesting to sing for Simon Cowell and see how *The X Factor* process worked. I just think it's for a certain type of person, which unfortunately isn't me.

Afterwards I prayed none of it would be on TV and I was so relieved when it wasn't. The only bit that got shown was a quick flash of me in a montage when I came out of the first audition screaming like a total moron. That was quite enough primetime TV embarrassment for me, thank you very much!

Later that year I started noticing I was getting ill a lot. I'd get a cough or a sore throat and it would linger. I just couldn't get rid of the cough but put it down to the fact I had been living in that mouldy and damp accommodation for so long before Rob and I had bought our first house.

I couldn't shake it and the thing is (to get technical for a moment) when you cough, your vocal cords slap together, and if you get a really bad cough then they're going to keep hitting each other and get very sore. If you can imagine, it's like having a pair of trainers on that are a size too small and your foot's rubbing and you end up getting a permanently throbbing blister.

When I get ill it really does affect my voice, but I would just sing through it. I ignored it for a while because I was younger and a bit more naïve back then. I would also feel bad because if I couldn't perform it meant someone had to cover for me and that makes their life harder. I always felt a big pressure not to say 'I can't sing tonight' because I didn't want to let anyone down. Part of the problem was that if you are the vocal coach or because you have such a strong voice people put you on a bit of a pedestal and never expect you to have a bad day.

So I'd carried on pushing it but I could feel I was messing up my vocal cords. I tried for as long as I could to blank it out but then the trepidation set in. It got to the point where I couldn't ignore it any longer, so I went to see my GP. However, he insisted it was just hayfever.

I so wanted to believe him, but I knew it wasn't as simple as that. 'But my voice isn't right,' I tried to explain. 'This is my career...' I added lamely. I didn't want to act like some kind of diva but this was my worst nightmare coming true. I was losing my voice.

The terror of this kept me badgering away until I managed to persuade him to refer me to an ENT (Ear, Nose and Throat) specialist. I was utterly terrified and starting to ask myself what would happen if I couldn't sing any more. If a singer loses their voice it's like a runner breaking his leg. Without my singing voice, I wouldn't know what to do with myself.

Obviously Whitney Houston lost her voice through the lifestyle she led. Mariah Carey also lost a lot of her range because she probably pushed it too much at her peak, which, through no fault of her own, damaged it. That happened with Adele too. She had nodules – little growths that appear on the vocal cords, affecting the voice – but she did the right thing and took a year out to get her voice back. It happens to so many singers because you constantly want to please and you constantly want to do what is expected of you and you feel bad if you ever say 'I can't today'. So you just keep doing it until you begin to wreck it. I'd heard so much about nodules and now I was convincing myself that was what was happening to me.

When I realised I'd have to wait three months to see an ENT specialist I flipped out and ended up paying to go private in order to see the same doctor a week later. I was expecting a proper examination and some answers, but this guy just asked me to open my mouth and literally looked down my throat for about five seconds and announced: 'You haven't got nodules, you're fine.' I replied, 'Well, I'm not fine, am I, or I wouldn't be here!' But he insisted it was just acid reflux and prescribed me something for that. I tried to protest but he had made his pronouncement and that was that, I was being ushered out. As I left I muttered angrily to myself, 'I know I haven't got acid reflux!'

He did do one positive thing, which was to refer me to a speech therapist. She got me to do all these different exercises, which I still do now. You probably wouldn't have ever seen me do it on *The Voice* but backstage I was always stretching my neck out, which is an exercise I learned from that therapist.

Because the ENT specialist had said I didn't have nodules I tried to convince myself my voice was simply becoming husky for no reason. But by now I could barely speak unless I was well lubricated. Even after trying to speak for a short period of time, I'd constantly need to be drinking water or else my throat would just dry up. This couldn't be right, surely?

I was still doing the shows every night and one time I was on stage singing 'Goldfinger' when I realised: 'I'm not going to be able to belt this out like I normally do.' It was a horrible moment of awareness – I was losing my natural ability to sing and it was physically hurting my throat. Having to constantly adjust and adapt the way I sang because I couldn't hit those big notes was bad enough, but to suddenly comprehend my voice was slipping away from me was both demoralising and scary.

My high voice was never affected; it was my belt voice, my chest voice, which seemed to be disappearing. It's the worst feeling in the world when the one thing that you're good at (and you get paid for) gets taken away from you.

It was such a frustrating time and I was constantly trying to push through and sing, but of course I was essentially just making it worse for myself. What should I do? I'd been told by the specialist I hadn't got nodules. At one point I even began to wonder if it was all in my head. Was it some sort of panic attack or anxiety-induced thing? Was I responsible for making myself ill? That thought was almost as frightening as nodules.

It was really stressful because all of a sudden I couldn't do what I normally do every night. This was my way of making a living, this is what made me happy, and it was slipping away from me and I was powerless to stop it. I'd lie awake at night worrying that my voice was never going to come back. In the morning I'd crawl out of bed exhausted, and panic that I was sounding even worse that day.

Eventually my speech therapist recommended another ENT consultant at the Norfolk and Norwich Hospital for a second opinion. This time my examination was much more in-depth – they put a camera on the end of a long tube, which went up my nose and back down my throat. It feels very uncomfortable and it really makes you gag, but then you can actually see the inside of your throat on a TV monitor. It was very weird but quite fascinating to see how it all works.

They got me to do an exercise to see how my vocal cords reacted on the screen when I sang and the doctor said, 'Your technique is really good.' I laughed: 'Thank God for that, because I'm a vocal coach too!' He explained it wasn't my technique that was causing my problem, and then stated, 'At the bottom of your vocal cords you've got two little marks which are the start of what could be nodules.'

It was as if he'd nudged me into an empty lift shaft and I felt myself fall. Nodules? Could this be the end of my singing career? He saw my stricken face and reassured me. 'It is the start of nodules. It's literally right at the very beginning. You've spotted it early on and with a bit of work on your part, you'll have your voice back soon.'

At that point I was so relieved I could have hugged him, I really could. I could have cried too but I still had a camera down my throat and after all that I didn't really want to make myself choke as well.

The relief washed over me as it sank in, and I knew I'd be all right. My voice would be OK, I could keep singing and music would stay a part of my life. I just don't know how I would have reacted if I'd been further down the line and I'd harmed myself for good. I don't know what I'd do if I wasn't singing; I've never done anything else. I'd probably need some serious therapy to get through that one. It wasn't the thought of not being able to perform on a stage that had been terrifying me the most; it was the fear of being unable to sing at all.

I get as much satisfaction singing in my attic on my own at home as I do on a stage in front of however many people. I've only ever done it for myself so if my voice was taken away from me, my whole world would come crashing in.

There's nothing you can prescribe to recover from the start of nodules. I had to continue with the speech therapy, use a steamer to clear my throat and sinuses regularly, drink loads of water and most important of all – rest.

What was harder was the change in lifestyle and it seemed like a lifetime while I was going through it. Over the space of the next six months to a year, I had to train my voice all over again, which was quite a lonely time because it meant I couldn't do anything. I couldn't go out, I couldn't socialise – you can't sit in a bar where it's too noisy because you'll try and talk over it. There were points when I'd think, 'Why the hell did I choose to become a singer?' Because you realise literally the whole world, everything you do, revolves around your voice. But even on my darkest, most boring and frustrating days, I knew there was nothing else I'd rather be doing.

Mentally I had to wrap my head around the change in lifestyle because it was quite extreme, but I kept reminding myself, 'The only person who can help you recover is you.'

I am incredibly thankful that I finally got to see a doctor who knew what he was talking about and spotted what was going on at an early stage. It's still scary to think what could have happened if no one had taken me seriously.

Around this time Billy, the manager I'd met in the US, got back in touch. He'd found me via Myspace and asked what I was up to, so I sent him a few songs I'd been working on, which he seemed to like. He went on to explain he was opening a big new blues club in Las Vegas at a Marriott Hotel and did I want to come over and work there for six months fronting his in-house band? I liked Billy and trusted him so there was no hesitation when I shot back a big: 'Yes please!'

He explained if I also signed a management deal with him, he'd get the right people to come and see me while I was out there and try and get me signed to a US record label. To be honest I wasn't bothered about a deal, I just loved the idea of being able to work in Vegas and being able to front a band, something I've always wanted to do. He could sort out a visa for Rob as well, which in all just made it too good an opportunity to walk away from. Although it was early days, Rob and I started planning to make it happen. I could ask about maybe getting a sabbatical from work; the house could be rented out; Mum and Dad agreed to have our Newfoundland dog Molly and our cats Jessie and Gizmo. We were excited, buzzing and I felt like nothing could go wrong this time around...

Except it did. The recession kicked in big time and with it went our Stateside dreams. Billy's financial backing fell through and the project got shelved. It was all such a let-down and felt like yet another knockback on an ever-growing list of career disappointments. I wasn't sure how much more I could take.

After that we settled into a more humdrum but contented rhythm and then came one of the happiest moments of my life, when Rob and I tied the knot in July 2011. It ended up being the hottest day of the year and was only a few months before I applied to be on *The Voice*.

We chose a beautiful big barn in the countryside near Norwich. Throughout all the planning and preparation, our one combined objective was, above anything else, to make it a fun day for all our friends and family. We had so much going on – there was an ice-cream man, a great soul band called The Bristol Johnson Experience, Willy Wonka-style chocolate favours, a pick 'n' mix sweet stand, and we had this great duo called Dumbfoundus – one of them plays bongos and the other one has a foot drum, a ukulele and kazoo. They are wicked!

Sometimes at Potters we'd get famous faces coming in to perform and Mel had secretly got some of them to record wedding messages for us. So it was hilarious to see the likes of Brian Conley, Joe McElderry, Len Goodman and Jane McDonald offering their congratulations when it was played at the end of the speeches, and it went down a storm with all of our guests.

Neither Rob nor I are slushy emotional types, which is also why we make a great team, but it was the perfect wedding day and everything we put into it was about making sure that everyone had a good time and so did we.

I don't understand why people go all psycho and Bridezilla when they get married. Why would you spend all that money to stress yourself out? It's not about getting stressed, or spending shed-loads of cash, is it? We were absolutely sweltering in the heat but standing there that evening, holding hands and watching all our friends and family grinning and swaying to the music, on the patio next to a field full of cows and sheep, made us both smile. Mainly with relief that it had all gone according to plan and everyone had enjoyed themselves, but also with happiness that we had each other.

All night people did keep asking me to get up and sing with the band but I would never do that at my own wedding. I know singers who have literally done a whole set at their wedding but it's not for me. This day was about Rob and I getting married and saying our vows together, not about me hogging the limelight with a microphone.

I didn't change my surname because I was already well known locally by my maiden name in my professional life and it seemed a shame to throw that away. However I did intend to double-barrel it and call myself Leanne Mitchell-Hurren. I'd got all the paperwork ready but then *The Voice* halted my intentions, because I couldn't then officially change my name halfway through the series.

For our honeymoon we went for eleven days to Mexico – we couldn't afford the whole two weeks! My memories of our time there are great. We did as much as we could – even swimming with dolphins, which was incredible – and stayed in a lovely resort. One of our favourite places to go out was Coco Bongos, which is a really famous and huge club in Cancun, a bit like Cirque Du Soleil. It had aerial performers and people zip-wiring above our heads. It was mental and surreal but totally brilliant. We loved every moment of being out there, just relaxing, laughing and having a good time.

We got back home loved-up, bronzed and stress-free, but I was brought back down to earth quite quickly and with a bump, when I was asked if I could go straight into work that day because half of the cast was off sick and they were struggling. So in I went.

But I was happy with my lot – I had Rob, my health and my music. I'd found a way to make music my life without the heartache that comes with trying to navigate your way through the hard edges of the music business. In a way I thought that was it; Potters was where I was destined to stay. I'd kind of accepted that and convinced myself this was as good as my singing career would get, and that was fine. At least that's what I was telling myself at the time. I had no idea my life was about to take a very unexpected turn indeed...

Chapter 5

Singing For My Life

It was around two months after our honeymoon that I first heard someone mention a TV show called *The Voice*. I was at home on a day off when my mobile started buzzing furiously. Glancing down I saw it was a text from my friend Caroline and the first thing that caught my eye was a flurry of exclamation marks. There must have been at least twenty of them: 'OMG have you heard of this new programme called The Voice?!!!!!!!!!!' it read. 'Have a look online!!! YOU HAVE TO AUDITION FOR IT!!!!!!!!!!!!!!!!!!!!!!!!!'

I didn't know what she was talking about and texted back saying as much, to which she replied instantaneously, 'Just do it!!!!!!!!!!!!!!', signing off with a trillion more of them. A steady stream of texts followed that one and in the end I flipped open my laptop and Googled it purely to shut her up.

I found a BBC website and started to read: 'Four of the biggest names in music are looking for incredible singing talent to compete for the title of *The Voice*. Only the most unique and distinctive voices will make it to the filmed auditions and get to sing for our celebrity coaches.' I scrolled down the page. 'Please only register for the open auditions if you are an artist with real talent and an amazing voice.'

The show had been a big hit in the States where Christina Aguilera was on the panel and the more I read the more interesting it sounded. Unlike all the other shows this one seemed to be about one thing and one thing only – your voice. Even the auditions were going to be blind, which was perfect for someone like me who gets self-conscious in new situations. All you had to do to apply was submit your email address, which I did – easy enough, tick, done it. And to be honest I didn't think much more of it.

I was in the middle of rehearsals for a massive Christmas show which not only had our whole theatre company in it, but also the entire Potters Theatre School, which numbers around 120 excitable kids. I'd also just taken over managing the team, so not only was I doing all the vocal arrangements and singing every night, I was now filling out time-sheets and organising staffing rotas as well. It was full on and my head felt ready to explode with it all. I was getting to the point where I didn't have a life any more because I was always working. I didn't really want to be a manager, but unfortunately there wasn't anyone else who could do it, so I'd reluctantly agreed to take on the role.

Nearly a month later when I got an email confirming my audition I'd almost forgotten all about it. But as I read on my heart sank. They couldn't have picked a worse date – the audition was on the same day as the opening night of our Christmas show! I didn't want to tell anyone about the audition at this stage because it would only add to the pressure of it all, but I knew they'd think I'd gone barking mad when I asked to take leave on the first night of a brand new show. Because I was now in charge I just booked myself off, but I was already thinking, 'This is going to be more hassle than it's worth,' and was at the point of giving up on *The Voice* before I'd even begun.

I've never been able to throw a sickie or anything like that because I hate lying, so when the show's producer, my friend Nicky, spotted I'd booked that day off I saw her face drop and I ended up blurting it all out. I then garbled that I was probably going to drop out anyway because I didn't want to let them down on such an important night. But Nicky said it was fine, insisted I went for it and agreed to keep mum: 'Look, we'll sort the understudies to cover for you. It's about time you put yourself out there...'

Even the night before the audition I still hadn't decided whether I was actually going or not. Rob kept saying, 'Just do it!', but a part of me was like, 'Can I be bothered to do this again?' It wasn't that I couldn't be bothered to try, it wasn't that at all. It was just that I always look at the reality of any situation and after my *X Factor* experience five years earlier, I was already convincing myself my chances of getting anywhere in this competition were somewhere between pretty slim and non-existent. Was I ready to put myself through that kind of disappointment again?

At that point I was just a name on a list for an open audition and no one knew if I could sing or not. I was effectively an email address to them and if I didn't go I wouldn't be letting anyone down, except maybe myself. I think the only reason I went for it in the end was because I thought, 'Let's just see if I can make myself do this.' It was my own personal challenge. Like, will you actually get off your bum, get out of your comfort zone and go to a bloody audition for once!

I got to sing every day for a living at Potters, so in that sense I was truly lucky. But by 2011 I'd been working there for thirteen years and much as I loved it, I had a niggling feeling that maybe there was more for me out there. I was still only twenty-seven – had I settled too early with my lot? Maybe it was time to grab one last opportunity before I actually was too over the hill and set in my ways.

Other than Nicky and Rob I hadn't told anyone about the audition, but the night before I was feeling bad about keeping my parents in the dark, so I called Mum and because she knows what I'm like I could hear her trying not to make too much fuss when I told her. But I can guarantee that as soon as she got off the phone she would have screamed to my dad: 'You won't believe this! She's auditioning!' They were both probably just a bit shocked I was actually going for something again. I asked Mum if she fancied coming to London to keep Rob company while I auditioned and she jumped at the chance.

The audition was at the Kingsway Hall Hotel in Covent Garden and I'd naïvely expected to just amble in, sing my song and nip home again. But as we turned on to the road we saw a giant queue winding around the corner into the next street. I was already thinking, 'This is my chance to get out of it,' so I started muttering: 'Let's just go and have a nice afternoon in London instead!'

What little confidence I had was rapidly starting to drain away – there were hundreds of people there. Loads of them had guitars and quite a few were listening to their iPods and humming along. 'I bet I won't even be seen now, looking at this lot...' I sighed. My nerves were jangling but because I never like to act nervous in front of my family or Rob, I tried to keep it light-hearted and joke about the fact that we were stood outside in the freezing cold, probably for nothing. I kept telling them to leave and go to Selfridges or somewhere, I'd just queue by myself. But they ignored me until we finally shuffled closer to the doors of the hotel. At this point they headed off because you weren't allowed to bring anyone into the actual audition with you.

Able to focus on the task in hand at last, I sat down in the hotel lobby, swigged down some water and took a deep breath. There were rows of chairs all filled with other auditionees, and as soon as I'd sat down some guy plonked himself down next to me and started rambling on about how he'd got really far in *Britain's Got Talent* and how he thought he was going to do really well on *The Voice* too.

'I don't want to blow my own trumpet but on *Britain's Got Talent*, I actually made it to the round before you get to audition for the judges and I reckon I'm going to do even better on *The Voice*,' he announced with such conviction that I couldn't help but smile. He was clearly the polar opposite of me. Sometimes people have so much self-belief whereas I could never imagine having that level of confidence. That said, I do sometimes wonder whether people say things like that because they really are full of self-assurance, or if it's just a case of the more they say it out loud the more they're trying to convince themselves as much as anyone else.

Eventually we were taken in groups of ten along what must have been the longest corridor in the world up to one of the hotel's conference rooms, which was all wood-panelling and swirly carpets. Sitting behind a desk was a guy with dreadlocks who I recognised as a vocal coach and alongside him one of the producers. We were instructed to stand in a row and one by one you had to take a step forward on to

After being crowned 'Miss Barbie' at Butlins Bognor Regis aged five (for one week only!).

Modelling for Eastern Electricity – he didn't have lenses in those glasses!

LEANNE MITCHELL
D.O.B. 14.12.83
Hair: Blonde
Eyes: Blue

That's my modelling card.

My first proper organ – I really was a cool kid!

'Send in the Clowns' aged 10 –
the first time I ever sang in public.
I look like a rabbit in headlights...

One of my regular local gigs –
aged 14 at the Red House pub in
Lowestoft.

My London debut... in Stringfellows!

Below: The photo the pubs used to publicise my gigs – where have my arms gone?

Top and Above: A few make up touch-ups during the never-ending photo shoot in San Francisco.

My face says
it all!

Below: The
red ensemble!
Shooting on the
beach in front of
the Golden Gate
Bridge.

Playing for San Fran music legend Pete Escovedo.

Me singing 'Pie Jesu' at Potters...

Opposite: ...And 'Anthem' from *Chess*.

Me and Rob
on our wedding
day in July 2011.

With my friends,
having a summer
picnic.

Team Tom –
before the
Battle Round.

Rehearsing 'Edge Of Glory' with Tom and Cerys Matthews.

This is what Mel gave me when I moved to London: wine, chocolate and a dodgy pic – perfect!

A final run-through for the Battles on set at Fountain Studios.

I can't believe it – I'm through to the live shows!

Going live for the first time and doing my best to get through 'Who Knew'!

Belting out 'I Put A Spell On You' in the third live show – I felt so much better with this performance.

Me and Tom being proper cool during the last week of the show!

I still can't believe I got to do this: duetting with Tom on 'Mama Told Me Not To Come'.

Flippin 'eck – I've only gone and won! Gobsmacked doesn't even begin to describe it...

Tom Jones is not only a legend, he's a true gentleman as well.

Above and right: At the 'Run to You' shoot – my first music video.

Chinwagging with Prince Harry – one of the most surreal moments of my life!

A snap taken at the recording studio, making the album!

Walking the red carpet for the first time at the National Television Awards 2013.

A sneak peek at my album artwork – I'm slowly getting used to photoshoots (helps to have an amazing photographer, thank you Simon).

the marker in front and sing your song. I was second from last so I had a long wait and my heart rate cranked up a gear each time the next singer stepped into pole position...

I had decided to sing Beyonce's 'Listen', which I'd never performed in public before. I'd sung it at home and loved it, but never had the guts to think I could get through this in front of an audience because it's such a hard song. But hey, why not throw yourself in at the deep end, Leanne? We'd been told to prepare a shortened ninety-second version for the audition so I'd chopped the first verse in half to get to the bridge into the chorus quickly, as normally the song is quite a slow starter. I wanted to make it my own a little bit but wasn't sure how it was going to come out. Most importantly I'd put the correct key into my phone so I could keep checking it, thinking, 'For God's sake, don't start too high or else you'll be screwed!'

One young girl in the line kept stopping because she didn't know her lyrics and had tears streaming down her face she was so nervous. I just wanted to go up to her, give her a big hug and say, 'Why are you putting yourself through this? You don't look like you're enjoying it...' I was only twenty-seven myself but I'd spent the last ten years looking after other singers and I don't like seeing people break down like that. I know what it feels like to be paralysed by fear, so when I see that in someone else I come over all maternal and just want to look after them.

The singer immediately before me was this grungy-looking girl and she stepped forward and asked, 'Is it OK if I swear?' They said that was fine so she started belting out Cee Lo Green's 'F*ck You'. She was good and I could see that the swearing comment and her in-your-face attitude would get her noticed. 'Damn,' I thought to myself. 'How can I fit a swear word into "Listen"?!'

Now it was my turn. I stepped forward and tried to be brave by looking at the two guys behind the desk in the eyes to make myself appear more confident, because after all these years as a singer I really knew I should be more confident by now. I'd been giving myself another pep talk as my turn approached: 'For God's sake, Leanne, you've done this long enough – get a grip!' Saying that, I was still terrified, I'm not going to lie. But I composed myself and began to do what I knew best: sing.

My other concern was the size of the room. It was quite small and I thought, 'Oh no, this is going to be really loud. I hope they don't think I'm shouting and that it doesn't just bounce back off the walls and deafen everyone.' But despite the nerves I also had an attitude of: 'Sod it. Stop worrying. You're here now so you might as well give it your all.' And that's what I did, and once I was into my professional stride, I felt more at ease.

There was a polite round of applause from everyone as I finished and when the final person had auditioned we were asked to stand outside the room, while they decided who would be going home. No one spoke as we awkwardly shuffled around in the corridor. The air crackled with tension. A couple of minutes later we were called back in and, like lambs to the slaughter, we lined up again.

I was so relieved when they said that I was through to the second round of auditions, to be held later that afternoon. Falling at the first hurdle would have been so demoralising and I would have felt really bad to have had to go back out to an excited Mum and Rob and tell them it was all over. What had also heartened me was that there'd been a vocal coach in the room, someone who could actually hear what you can do and the potential in your voice, as opposed to just a producer who's looking at you from a totally different perspective altogether. They also gave a really encouraging speech to the people who hadn't made it through. Rather than just saying, 'You're out, see ya,' they took time to make sure everyone was OK and to check that they'd had a positive experience.

Next I was taken (with one other person from our group – the 'F*ck You' singer) to a waiting area where the others who'd got through were gathered. People were chatting to each other but I'm always a bit shy in these situations so I sat slightly apart from the others. I think I was one of the last to be seen that day, if not the last. Soon I was pretty much sat there on my own. Eventually I was taken to another floor and instructed to wait on a solitary chair by a door in the corridor. It was like being a naughty schoolkid who'd been sent to see the headmaster. I felt so strange at this point; I was still nervous as I knew I had to sing again, but at the same time I was so excited. I was being given a chance and I didn't want to mess it up!

Eventually I was taken inside what was one of the hotel's chintzy bedrooms and sitting in two little armchairs were a vocal coach, who introduced himself as Mark de Lisser, and alongside him a producer. It's funny because I thought Mark looked really scary, whereas I later found out he's actually one of the smiliest, nicest guys you could meet. But that day he obviously had his poker face on and neither of them gave anything away as I sang Beyonce's 'If I Were A Boy' and 'Hurt' by Christina Aguilera. We were only supposed to do a minute and a half but they didn't stop me so I just kept going. Thank God I knew the whole songs.

After I finished they asked me to take a seat back in the corridor while they made a decision. I was just about to leave the room when Mark asked me how long I had been singing. 'Forever,' I replied and he just nodded sagely and wrote something down. God knows what!

Outside, as I perched back on the chair I hadn't a clue how it had gone but felt happy with my vocals and didn't think I'd let myself down. Before I had time to over-analyse the situation and start picking apart what I could have done better, one of the show's production runners came bounding towards me and led the way down the corridor asking me about what I'd done in the past and chattering away nineteen to the dozen. Then she suddenly exclaimed, 'Oh silly me, I forgot to say, you've got through, by the way!' I was chuffed to bits and a grin quickly spread across my face. She added: 'There's no more singing left today – all you've got to do now is an interview and then that's it.'

Back in the waiting area a giddy combination of adrenaline and nerves churned in my stomach. For the interview they stood me in front of a camera and asked me questions about my favourite artists, how I got into singing and the deal that had gone pear-shaped when I was younger. Then that was it, I was free to go and I think I was literally the last person that walked out of the auditions that day.

I was taken back down to the lobby where Mum and Rob were now waiting and I was handed a piece of paper with dates on and told I'd hear in the next week or so if I'd made it through to the call-backs (the last round before the televised blind auditions). As we were driving home, Mel, who'd been at work, started texting me asking where I was as she'd spotted I hadn't been at Potters for the show that night. She'd put two and two together as to why I'd taken such a random day off and just screamed down the phone like a madwoman when I confirmed what she'd already guessed. But as usual I was playing it cool – if I got a call-back then I'd allow myself to get excited!

A few days later I was in the dressing room at Potters when my phone rang. I could see it was a blocked number and for some reason I just knew it was going to be about *The Voice*. I took a deep breath and picked up. I was right; it was a producer and he had good news – I was through to the call-backs! He said out of the 28,000 people who had auditioned, there were only 250 singers that had actually got the call-back and that number would be halved again, down to around 100 for the actual blind auditions. Oh my God! It was getting serious now! But I still didn't let myself think too far ahead as to what it would actually mean if I did get through...

An email confirmation arrived a couple of hours later: 'Dear Leanne, as discussed on the phone we are delighted to invite you to a call-back audition for our exciting new BBC1 show, *The Voice*. Congratulations on impressing the producers and vocal coaches so far. Only a small percentage of auditionees we met have been invited to this final stage so you should be very proud of yourself. Your call-back audition is 13 December at 11:00. The session will last about three hours.' That was the day before my birthday. 'Could that be a good sign?', I thought to myself randomly.

The email asked me to pick my favourite songs from a list and to write them down in order of preference, and to make sure I included a selection of up-tempo, mid-tempo or slow songs. It explained that there'd be lots of activities on the day of the call-back, including a session with a vocal coach and a chat with a doctor to make sure that each of us would be able to handle the potential pressures of filming a TV talent show.

'...Come dressed as you wish to represent yourself as an artist. Well done again and we look forward to seeing you at the call-backs.'

Blimey, there was so much to take in and as I re-read everything I realised that also attached were various legal documents, participation agreements, rules, a personal disclosure form, health declaration form... The list went on and on and it also stated that everything had to be completed and returned by midnight the next day. And on top of that I had to find something decent to wear!

I was going to need some help with this lot so I quickly rang Mel. 'I've literally got twenty-four hours to pick these songs!' I explained. 'Right, I'm coming over and we are going to sort this out,' she replied, taking control. 'Have you got a bottle of wine?' So we necked a much-needed glass of rosé while I highlighted all the songs I'd consider singing, then Mel and I put them in order of preference as instructed and we emailed everything back to the BBC.

A few days later I received another call saying that having looked at my song list they wanted me to sing 'If I Were A Boy' and Aretha Franklin's 'Respect' at the audition. I was happy with both of these choices. For 'If I Were A Boy' I'd just sing the first verse and chorus I'd prepared for the open audition, and I'd sung 'Respect' at work so I managed to dig out an old backing track. Plus they said I could choose another song myself and I opted for 'Hurt' as that had seemed to go down OK first time around.

My music was all sorted, now all I had to worry about was my voice. The weekend before the call-backs I'd managed to get a really bad cold and could barely speak. 'This is so typical,' I croaked to Rob. 'Finally I get through to something and then this happens. I won't be able to get on *The Voice* because I haven't got a bloody voice!' So I just did what I normally do in those situations: tried not so speak unless I had to, rested, regularly used a steamer to clear my throat and sinuses, drank plenty of water and hoped for the best!

The call-backs were at a recording studio and rehearsal space called The Joint, which is just around the corner from King's Cross Station in London. I was full of cold and constantly sucking on throat sweets – I must have gone through a whole packet on my way down there that morning. I didn't worry too much about what I was wearing and just made myself look presentable; this show was about 'The Voice' after all.

At The Joint there was a general buzz of nerves in the air and I sat in the waiting area praying my voice would hold out because I had three really belty numbers to get through.

My warm-up was with vocal coach, Jay Henry, who as a singer has worked with some amazing artists himself, including one of my idols, Mariah Carey. Jay took me into one of The Joint's little vocal booths and I told him about my cold. He suggested I sing a bit of 'Respect' for him and when I was done he gave me a big smile. 'God, you can sing!' he laughed, which was a relief to hear. While I knew he was more than likely saying that to everyone as a bit of a confidence boost, it did the trick for me. Although I thought I still sounded pretty bunged-up, there wasn't much I could do about it and I just hoped technique would help me through.

Waiting to go into the audition I drank bucket-loads of water in an attempt to keep my voice lubricated. Not that that was unusual, I'm always like that with water especially when I'm singing. As soon as I emptied one bottle I asked the production team, 'Excuse me, have you got another water, please?' I was constantly asking – I must have drunk about three litres of water before I went into the audition at eleven o'clock that morning. I was needing to pee every five seconds as well!

This time there were about ten people on sofas making notes in a much bigger rehearsal room, and in front of them was a tiny stage with a mike stand on it. Everyone seemed much friendlier this time around and I got the feeling they were trying to put everyone at ease. As I sang my voice held and I felt a huge sense of relief that I'd got through it without anyone shielding their ears in pain.

After that it was the one-on-one 'getting to know you' meeting with a producer who explained the rules and outlined what would be expected from us if we got through. She was really no-nonsense and stated that while they would do everything they could to help the contestants, they wouldn't stand for divas or anyone acting up on this show.

You know when you feel like you're being told off before you've even done anything wrong? So I started laughing nervously at this point and tried to explain to her that I really wasn't the diva type. 'I'm just happy to be here,' I insisted, but at the same time thinking this was a really random conversation to be having. Shouldn't we just see how today went first before we started thinking too far ahead?

Next was my chat with the doctor, which involved a fifteen-minute walk up the road to the offices of Wall to Wall television, the production company who were making the show for the BBC. I wasn't even worrying about what this session was going to entail, because I was now fully focused on the fact I stupidly had these really high heels on and nobody had told me we'd have to walk for ages on a higgledy-piggledy cobbled street, which was a challenge in itself. Now my feet were killing me and I had to use all my concentration on trying not to fall arse over tit. Maybe this was all just part of the personality test?

Eventually I was shown into a sparsely decorated office and sitting there was a really tall guy who had the most massive hands I'd ever seen. You know when doctors use their hands a lot when they talk? Well, that's what he was doing and I was literally transfixed by them. They were like spades on the end of his arms and I couldn't tear my eyes away. Again the session was quite random and I was a bit bemused by the whole experience!

He said he was a psychiatrist and began: 'At the moment obviously you're nobody, you can walk up the street and no one's going to look twice. But if you get through, suddenly everyone will be staring at you going, "OH MY GOD, IT'S LEANNE!"' He shouted that last bit so loudly it actually made me jump. So I was relieved when he lowered his voice again and continued with a series of fairly straightforward questions.

In the car home I mulled the day over and realised I hadn't a clue how it had gone. But I did feel positive, that I'd done all I could and now it was completely out of my hands.

A week had gone by and I was at home on the day before Christmas Eve when I got the call. 'Basically we want to let you know that we were all completely blown away with your audition and you're through!' said the producer. My stomach somersaulted – I couldn't believe it! He said they'd be in touch about rehearsal dates, I managed to mumble 'thank you' a few times and that was that.

I was totally gobsmacked and put the phone down thinking, 'Oh God, now what do I do? Should I call someone?' In the end it was Mel because Rob was at work and I couldn't get hold of him – she just screamed down the phone at me of course! I also let Mum and Dad know. However, I kept the phone calls short and sweet. I needed a few moments to digest this information. I was taking it all in and as ever I needed to think everything through logically before I threw myself into it. I'm not the most excitable of people, but I could feel the tingle of exhilaration burning inside of me. I'd been given another chance to further my love of music, to challenge myself and show what I could do to a whole new audience – and this time, maybe for the first time, I felt like I was in safe hands.

So then I had this huge secret to carry around. I needed to keep it to myself for my own sanity, as I was still getting my own head round it and wanted to see how I got on before I started telling the world. It's funny because on Christmas Day Rob gave me this cute little Pandora charm that had 'Good Luck' inscribed on it, and when I went in to do the show that night some of the girls asked me what I'd got for Christmas. 'Rob bought me this charm,' I said, holding out my wrist with the bracelet on it. One of them came up to me and read it: 'Good luck? What's that for then?' I flashed her my best poker face. 'Oh, nothing special,' I replied. But at the same time I couldn't resist a secret little smile to myself.

It's funny, because at the time, all I had really got to was the first round, the blind audition, but to me this was a massive achievement. There was no turning back now and I wouldn't have wanted to anyway. I can honestly say that so far – minus the spade-handed doctor perhaps – I had enjoyed every second and for me that was a big deal. Even if this was as far as I would get, it really had given me a confidence boost. Not necessarily in my ability, but in knowing that I could push myself, and in doing so I could achieve something. The only difference was that now I had to impress a whole new set of people that hadn't heard me before and didn't know anything about me – and these people were about as famous as you could get!

Chapter 6

Blind Ambition

The rehearsal dates for the blind auditions were drawing nearer and speculation was at fever pitch as to who the coaches were going to be. The grapevine was ablaze with rumours, whispers and excited chatter as a long tally of A-list artists were bandied about. Every day there was a new name mooted in the press, but the first to be officially confirmed was Jessie J. I thought she was a brilliant singer and a superb choice. Not only did she have an incredible voice, she had credibility as a songwriter with bags of talent. I remember watching her on YouTube singing 'Mama Knows Best', sat in her bedroom before she'd even been signed, and thinking she was going to make it big.

I knew if she was on the panel, this show was going to have credibility. And the release of the next name was added testament to this: Danny O'Donoghue from The

Script. I was a big fan of his so I was really thrilled to bits.

He'd made a fair impression on me when I'd seen him with The Script, supporting Take That at Wembley Stadium a year or two earlier. He was in the middle of their hit 'Breakeven (Falling To Pieces)', when he suddenly stopped and let the crowd sing it instead. He sat down on the side of the stage as the audience chanted it, shaking his head in disbelief and seeming completely overwhelmed by the fact that this whole stadium was singing his song back to him. As I watched I felt quite emotional for him and I remember thinking, 'God, what must that feeling be like? It's not even your own concert, it's Take That's concert, and yet the crowd absolutely love you!'

Following these two, will.i.am from the Black Eyed Peas was confirmed, which I thought was a great choice because he is so big in all fields of the industry. And finally, of course, there was Tom Jones! Tom Jones, with his huge voice, amazing charisma, incredible career and decades of hits and re-inventions. Someone for whom the words 'Living Legend' really do apply.

I thought they'd got the mix completely right – the coaches were fun, knowledgeable and all massively talented. All of it was on course to be something of which anyone would be proud to take part, except that was the bit I couldn't quite wrap my head around. I couldn't imagine at any point I was going to be standing there singing in front of these four megastars – or to the backs of their chairs at the very least! That terrifying thought was so off the grid that in order to cope I pushed it to the back of my mind and instead focused on the task in hand – the rehearsals.

'Your first rehearsal is on Saturday 7 January at 10.15 a.m...' This was my confirmation email and I read it for the hundredth time that day at least. The location was The Joint again so at least I knew where I was going. The email went on to explain that I'd have a rehearsal with the house band (which I was very excited about!), plus sessions with a vocal coach, a choreographer and a stylist. There it was in black and white – this was really happening and I hadn't dreamt it all!

I had a total of three rehearsal sessions to prepare for the Blinds – as the blind auditions were called – and was feeling a mixture of excitement and fear, but what made it worse was not being able to tell people. Booking time off work was tricky because I was taking random days off in the middle of January (who takes time off in January?) and each time I mumbled some vague excuse. Obviously, I could have told some work colleagues and friends who would have kept it a secret, but I couldn't have handled the pressure of everyone knowing and therefore asking me all the time how it was going. So I just tried to keep it to myself for as long as I could, which was hard for me as I hate lying and I'm not very good at it either!

The song they wanted me to sing at the Blinds was 'If I Were A Boy' again and they emailed me the edit of it, which was pretty much a verse and a chorus and what I'd been doing anyway, so at least there wasn't a worry for me of having to learn a brand new song.

I had no idea what to expect at the first rehearsal but I have to admit I felt really excited to be doing it with a full live band, something I'd always wanted to do. The location was familiar as it was the same room I'd been in for the call-backs, and as I walked in and saw the band all set up and ready to go, my heart soared and I knew this was going to be a lot of fun.

All of the guys in the band introduced themselves to me including Steve Sidwell, the musical director. They all seemed really nice and had so much experience between them, playing with everyone from Amy Winehouse and Robbie Williams to Eric Clapton and Shirley Bassey. These were the best in the business and I felt really honoured to have the chance to perform with them.

They asked me what key I wanted to sing in and I told them the original would be fine, and they played it through once for me to listen to so I could get the feel of it. Then I was thrown in at the deep end and it was my turn to sing. I held on to the mike and just went for it.

I had sung with a band at Potters, but the band there is in a different area to the performers, and not on stage with you so it didn't feel the same. I thought it was great *The Voice* was doing it this way. By using a live band, you knew this was going to be a proper quality show, with the emphasis on the music.

This was also the first time I met my vocal coach for the whole series, Yvie Burnett. I recognised her straight away because she's worked on so many other TV shows and is well respected in the industry. After the band rehearsal, she took me into another room to work on the song together. The band had recorded my rehearsal through the sound desk and had given me a USB stick to listen back to with Yvie. I usually find things like this very hard, because I don't like hearing recordings of myself with other people listening in.

Thankfully it was only a short session but it was also very helpful. Together we went through my vocal bit by bit. The first thing Yvie told me was as you begin singing you need to sniff and breathe in through your nose, which basically lifts up the muscles in your face. She called this technique 'smelling a rose' – I'd learnt something new already!

Next I had a slot with the choreographer to talk about my general stage presence. I had to perform the song to her and to myself in front of a full-length mirror – which is pretty much my worst nightmare. I know for some people it really helps watching themselves as they perform a song, but I hate it. It makes me over-think what I'm doing and

I'd rather not know what weird faces I'm pulling! 'Bloody hell, that's a big voice!' she laughed when I started, which tended to be everyone's initial reaction to me on *The Voice*. My lack of confidence would then make a reappearance as my own reaction to that tended to be: 'Uh-oh, is that a good thing or a bad thing?'

The choreographer kept telling me, 'Open your eyes so you can connect with the audience!' I joked and said, 'I will when there is an audience, I can't do it to just me!' She was good at confidence-boosting though, helping me think about how I was going to perform it, rather than just going out and winging it.

But I didn't want to have anything 'choreographed' as such. It may sound odd, but for me, once you become aware of what you're doing you feel like you need to Perform with a capital P, and I'm not like that. I don't like having choreographed movements because it all feels a bit fake and unnatural. I just do what feels right when I'm lost in the song and I don't really enjoy dissecting it.

I know it's not the same for all singers, and it's a case of each to their own. Some of the others loved having choreography, especially the ones with a dancing background. I remember when we did a group number further down the line and one of the other artists started doing pirouettes in the middle of the room during rehearsal. It's always like that for dancers – back at Potters any time we were in a rehearsal some of them couldn't resist doing a few high leg kicks to pass the time. Needless to say, I wasn't one of them!

Next I had to go and see Faye Sawyer who was the fashion stylist for the show. I had tried to make an effort to look presentable. We'd been instructed to bring along three outfits and when I showed the clothes to her, she asked: 'Are they all black?' To which I had to confess most of them were. She rolled her eyes and laughed. 'Everyone wants to wear bloody black – you're not allowed to wear black!' I wasn't sure what to say to that and was hoping she wasn't going to say I had to wear some brightly coloured outfit that I'd feel ridiculous in.

Luckily she actually said the complete opposite, telling me that I should wear something I feel comfortable in, preferably with a bit of colour in there somewhere. So I decided on a long black top over skinny jeans finished off with a short rusty-red kimono top. They also asked me how I wanted to have my hair – big and curly please! I really wanted to just be myself so I could feel moderately comfortable in an otherwise terrifying environment. To my immense relief, Faye was lovely; she understood this and was on my side. As the show went on, I became a lot closer to Faye. She is an amazing person and soon became one of my closest confidantes on the show.

I felt really positive and buoyant when I journeyed home to Lowestoft that afternoon. And as you may have realised by now, for me to honestly feel like I've really enjoyed something is quite an achievement and so that was an extra-special day. I was relishing the rehearsals and enjoying the novelty of living just in the moment. It had not hit home all this was leading up to singing and being judged on national TV. All my brain would allow me to process was what a great experience I was having and the money-can't-buy advice I was being given by all these professionals.

A couple of days later I had another vocal session with Yvie. This was the point where we had more time to get to know each other and when she started to see what I could do. She'd got a keyboard set up and said, 'Right, let's start with some scales and I can have a listen to your voice.'

So that was when I did a first proper set of scales with her. I just had to hum and keep going up and up and up, higher and higher, and then you could sort of see her eyes widening and she went, 'Oh my God – your range! People just don't sing that high!' I was taken aback by her reaction because I'm so used to my own voice; I'd never heard anything remarkable in it. It wasn't that I could sing higher than anyone she'd ever heard or anything, I guess it was just that not a lot of pop singers would have that higher register, as maybe they hadn't been trained to find it. Personally I think everyone has an 'opera voice' in there somewhere!

While inwardly I was beaming at the fact she seemed so impressed, I was also slightly apprehensive when she said we needed to work all those notes into the song. The point she made was, because I only had a minute and a half to show what I could do, I'd got to include things that I wouldn't necessarily normally do within such a short space of time. She instilled in me the importance of literally giving it your all. So we started singing it through and working out some higher notes, which she seemed to love. I put my trust in Yvie and I really liked having someone to guide and help me for a change, because I was so used to it being the other way around at Potters.

All thoughts of TV appearances were shut down and locked away in a box marked 'DO NOT EVEN THINK ABOUT IT'! At that point, if I'd had even the slightest clue of just how massive the show was going to be, and how many millions would be watching, I would have gone into meltdown and become a gibbering wreck there and then. So far I was totally absorbed by and loving the whole rehearsal process. Here I was, working with some of the best and most experienced people in the music business and learning so much from their knowledge. This was already like winning the top prize for me.

However the pressure stepped up a gear the following week. The final rehearsal was going to be at the BBC Studios in London, somewhere I'd seen a million times on TV shows I'd grown up with like *Blue Peter*, *Live & Kicking* and *Children In Need*. It was going to be totally surreal to actually be there! I'd been told I'd be working with my vocal coach and the band again, and that I'd also be having my very first interview on camera which would probably be used in the final show.

The enormity of it all started to dawn on me as I sat in the busy imposing reception at BBC TV Centre and felt the thumping of my heart in my chest. Up until now I'd been having a great time – I was being vocal coached, singing with a band, getting good style tips – but now the reason why all this was happening was too big to ignore. I was going to be on TV singing in front of four superstars, with a live studio audience for a show that would be going out to millions of primetime viewers. It was almost too much to comprehend.

That morning I'd wanted to arrive at the BBC relaxed, prepared, in control and on time. Instead the opposite happened. Rob and I had driven to a tube station on the outskirts of London and, as I had to be ready before I arrived, I had got in the car with my extensions in, my hair all curled, full make-up on, outfit on – four hours before I was even due to rehearse.

As I clambered on to the crowded tube, an announcement boomed out informing everyone of delays on the line. So I stood there getting increasingly hot, my make-up melting off, my feet aching, my hair going lank and my stress levels rising. Finally I arrived late and flustered, and barely had time to catch my breath in reception before I was rushed through security via a maze of corridors and stairways until I got to Yvie who was waiting for me outside the doors of Studio 1.

She took my arm and gave me some words of encouragement. I could tell she was trying to keep me calm but I think she was also panicked that I was late because they were obviously trying to run to a tight schedule.

I was taken straight on to the set and this huge new space amazed me the first time I saw it. There was so much to take in: people scurrying around; the set itself, which was still being built around us; cameras everywhere; microphones; and all these seats – flippin 'eck – all these seats! I could scarcely believe there were so many and that they would eventually all be filled with people.

What also grabbed my attention and brought home the reality of it all was a huge red chair. At that point there was just the one chair in place with gaps for the others, but I knew that soon a famous person would be sitting in that and listening to me sing. Adding to the enormity of it all was the silver sculpture of a giant fist holding a microphone – a huge replica of *The Voice*'s trophy. A little voice in me squeaked, 'Oh my gosh – this is big!'

There was a deluge of noise filling the space: producers telling me about the sound, someone talking to me about the band, the chatter of stage directions. My head was whirring. I felt like I was on a merry-go-round and could barely hold on. I sternly told myself to calm down, breathe, and go with the flow.

After each run-through of the song Yvie came up to me, asked how I felt and gave me a few pointers. Also the sound guy kept coming up to me asking me if I was okay, if I needed anything changing with the vocal or the sound levels ... this was something I was not used to! I've worked with quite a few sound engineers in my years of performing and they certainly are not all that accommodating!

I was fine with it all and at the last attempt Yvie suggested trying it with all those high notes we'd practised – just to give it a go. I really didn't want to but reminded myself 'Go with the flow' and took those notes to their highest point possible. Afterwards Yvie bounded up to the stage and excitedly told me the producers loved it so much they wanted me to keep them in. I was stunned and realised I had just made things much harder for myself!

Being on the set for the first time was a fairly daunting moment because you feel like everybody's looking at you and judging you, and so all you've got in your head is 'Don't mess it up and try and do your best'. I was really trying to act like I was confident but I bet it didn't come across like that. Looking back I'm pretty sure I looked and acted like a scared little mouse who wanted to run for the hills.

However I do know it wasn't just me. Being in an environment like that for the first time was intimidating for all of us and anybody who says it wouldn't affect them is either ridiculously arrogant, supremely confident, thick-skinned or they are just lying. It doesn't matter how much experience you've got – I've been performing since I was ten years old but it's a completely different ball game doing it with cameras in your face. The pressure felt massive and this was just the rehearsal, there wasn't even a studio audience in there yet...

The other thing I had to worry about was the actual stage, and the physical implications of getting on and off. It had a shiny floor surface, which was really slippery. I was wearing higher shoes than I'd ever worn before and every time I took a step a voice in my head was screaming: 'Don't fall over, don't fall over!'

Then if that wasn't bad enough, around the edge of it you've got this sort of grille with little holes in it, under which lie the sound monitors. But the grille holes are just about the right size to fit your stiletto down, which I think later in the show Barbara Bryceland did at one point. She got her foot stuck, but luckily it was only in rehearsals.

As I left the studio through the doors I heard another auditionee singing Stevie Wonder's 'Superstition' – it was David Faulkner who got through to the Battle rounds – and I thought, 'Bloody hell, he's amazing.' I knew then the standard was going to be high. Meanwhile I was whisked off to do an interview in another studio in front of a screen with *The Voice*'s logo on it. The camera, which was on a runner, was going round and round as they fired questions at me. It felt so odd having to stand there dead still and talk about myself while this camera was spinning all over the place and circling me.

They kept asking the question – which coach do you want to turn around? Who would you pick? And I kept on refusing to answer because quite genuinely I didn't have a preference. I simply and honestly wouldn't have minded which one it was. I'd be happy if any of them turned around. It would be beyond my wildest dreams to be acknowledged by any of them. It was as simple as that.

And that was it – that was the end of the rehearsals. The next one was the big one, the actual blind audition! At home I started thinking, 'How am I going to feel if no one turns around? Am I going to feel humiliated?' Because I think that was kind of the biggest thing for me: 'How is this going to look if I get shown on TV and no one turns around?' Because everything I'd done up until now – all the auditions I'd got through, as much fun as I'd had and as great as this process had been – it meant nothing. I realised with a sickening thud that it was all hinging on this audition.

I was still at work and it was great to be able to take my mind off *The Voice* for a few days. But sometimes in a quiet moment, the thought of me standing on that stage would loom into my mind and all I could see was the back of a row of red chairs and a deadly silence as no one moved. It was like visualising my worst-case scenario, and what made me white with fear was realising this could be a reality very soon.

The second I woke up on the day of the Blinds, I sat bolt upright and thought, 'This is it, it's make or break time!' I was allowed to bring three members of my family or friends and we'd been told they'd be on camera and would be interviewed as well. Rob, Mum and Dad were coming with me and in some ways this helped at first because I could put my own nerves to one side whilst I listened to their mini-dramas. My parents were very excited but Mum was fretting about what to wear as usual and, even more importantly, what was she going to put my dad in. What would they say in front of the camera, how would they look, what would they need to do to their hair? Meanwhile Rob was quietly breaking into a cold sweat at the thought of being on telly. He admitted he was more nervous that day than he was at our wedding.

They'd put us all up in a hotel in west London the night before because we had to be at BBC TV Centre by 8 a.m. When we got inside everything was very secret squirrel because there were all of us singers and they had to keep us away from the celebrity coaches. They didn't want any of us bumping into them at any point before the blind audition.

For most of the day we were hidden away in a different building altogether, which was just down the road from TV Centre. In the holding area there were lots of little groups of families and I whiled away the hours trying to guess who were the singers and who were their guests.

Rob, my parents and I sat together for ages, which didn't help my stress levels at all because by now their nerves were starting to rub off on me. I'm not very good with them being around in those kinds of situations and I'd rather just be by myself.

But obviously I tried to act like I was fine. The producers kept saying to me all day, 'You seem so laid back and cool,' and I would reply, 'Well, that's the way I'm acting, yeah, because I don't want this lot to get any worse.' Whereas underneath I was so nervous I wanted to run out of that door screaming!

When the show's presenters Holly Willoughby and Reggie Yates suddenly appeared and were getting ready to start interviewing some of the other people, I was like, 'Oh my God, this is really happening!' Their presence was bringing it all one step closer.

Then I was filmed walking in with my family and Rob made me laugh out loud for the first time that day when he whispered, 'Leanne! How should I walk?' We all had to try and act naturally as we walked down a red carpet outside, past this weird little water feature and then entered the building in single file. At one point Mum messed it up when the door was apparently too heavy for her to push open. She stood there struggling for a second before the camera guys started laughing and asked us to do it again.

Next was our interview with Reggie back in the holding area. Earlier I'd seen someone else doing her interview – I later found she was called Aundrea Nyle – and she had her little girl with her. She'd appeared so confident and bubbly, it made me shrink a little. 'Oh no, I haven't got to be like that, have I?' I thought. I could feel the nerves beginning to take over and my throat starting to get dry.

Thank goodness for Reggie Yates at that point. He really was lovely and achieved mission impossible by putting us all at our ease. He even managed to help me not sound like a total prat. Despite this I knew my dad was going to come out with something stupid in a minute. Which he did. He started telling Reggie how he was into cars and that he was about to buy an old Ferarri ... oh my God, Dad, not the time!

Reggie could see Rob looked completely terrified and said to him, 'Are you nervous?' 'A little bit,' replied Rob. Reggie asked him to hold out his hand and it was actually shaking all over the place.

When I saw that, I felt such a pang of responsibility towards Rob and my parents. They had always been so supportive of me and here they were, genuinely beside themselves with nerves. It hit me then it was a physical and mental pressure on them as well. I was worried not just for myself, but also about them. What were they going to be like if I didn't get through? They were investing so much in this and they had such blind faith in me; I didn't want to let them down because they were so confident in my abilities. I'd be gutted for them more than me if I didn't get through. Even though it would be a huge disappointment I knew I could handle it, but how would they react? Could they handle it?

But I had no time to dwell on that right now. My immediate concern was my mounting terror about the blind auditions. However, I was also trying to get in the mindset that if I didn't get through, I wasn't going to regret entering altogether as it really had started to boost my confidence and had been such a great experience.

At around 2 p.m. I was taken to the studio and I was happy to go. I needed to be on my own in order to focus and concentrate on what I was there for. In the meantime my family would be filmed watching my audition on a screen in a room backstage with Reggie.

About ten of us were driven in a minibus around the corner to the main BBC building and suddenly we saw this massive queue of people lining up to be in the studio audience. It snaked all the way down the road. As my eyes followed its long path, my adrenaline really started to kick in and all I could think and mutter to myself was 'Oh. My. God...'

We were led into the Star Bar, which was another waiting area, and I got chatting to some of the other singers. I met Aundrea who was really friendly and talkative. I also spoke to Joelle Moses, who was asking me who I'd pick but again I said I didn't know. I'd met Bill Downs before at the call-backs – he's a really nice, laid-back (and talented) guy from Norwich, so it was great to see a familiar face in there too.

Nathan James, the guy who ended up going on that ITV *Superstar* programme, was there too. He seemed very confident and had a few others huddled around him. Stood next to him was a girl who I think was in musicals and warmed up by kicking her leg up in the air and doing some stretching. A guy with a big grey beard and a woman with a brown bob were in a corner practising their harmonies over and over again, which I later found out is what the lovely Matt and Sueleen do about a thousand times before they go on. I think they definitely should win the prize for the most rehearsed act of the show!

We had to wait at least an hour and a half in there and it was really weird because we were constantly on lock-down when the coaches were around, so nobody was allowed to go in or out unescorted in case you bumped into them. Even if you wanted the loo you had to ask permission and be taken at a specific time when it was safe. As the tension began to mount, you could cut the atmosphere with a knife.

At one point I was taken for a warm-up in an empty dressing room with Yvie. She told me to just go for it and said she thought I'd go far. I mumbled, 'Oh, I don't know.' And she went: 'I'm telling you, I'll be seeing you in six weeks and I'll be saying I told you so!' So that was a fantastic and well-timed confidence booster from Yvie, who was really sweet and was another person I really clicked with. However by this point the nerves had set in to such an extent that I honestly didn't believe a word of it because I had now heard and seen some of the other singers and knew how good they all were.

I was one of the first group to be taken backstage where we were all given a little pep talk by the same scary producer who'd warned us not to act like divas at the call-backs. Then it was time for the show to start and we all turned our attention to a TV screen backstage, not wanting to miss a second. First up was Aundrea doing 'Crazy' and she was so sassy, confident and soulful that it felt right when Tom turned around. Bang! That was the first place gone.

Everyone was delighted for her but also as the auditions went on, it seemed to us nervously waiting in the wings that the coaches were turning around a lot. I convinced myself they'd be told to not be so trigger-happy just before I went on – after all, they could each only pick ten singers for their team.

They'd turned around for Joelle too and I was really worried they were going to start getting picky when they realised they hadn't even got the first ten out of the way yet and they'd still got 100 more auditions to get through.

Having to watch what was happening on a TV screen was excruciating and made it so much worse, because by now I was thinking, 'I've got to do that in a minute,' and then you have no choice but to start comparing yourself to everyone that has gone before. It was a case of: 'Well, she was great, why did no one turn around for her?'

When they finally called my name, I thought my already thumping heart was going to explode. As we walked towards the 'Blue Room', which is the backstage area where on TV you saw us being filmed as we're preparing to walk on stage, my head was swimming and I became aware my mouth was drier than a desert. I took another glug of water and then suddenly someone whisked the bottle out of my sweaty hand. I stood there open-mouthed and panicky but stupidly didn't think to ask them if I could keep it. It was so hot and dry in there, I was convinced my voice was about to give up on me.

When I'm doing a show, in the space of an hour I can easily get through over two litres of water. I drink water by the bucket. I think that's what I was mostly known for by the producers who would take us to the side of the stage on *The Voice*. I'd always make sure they had water there, because I'd totally panic if my bottle ran out before I went on.

However, at the Blinds when they took that last bottle away from me, they inadvertently did me a favour. It almost took my mind off what was waiting for me on the other side of that door, because I was so busy focusing my attention on this sudden lack of water rather than what was about to happen next.

Then all at once, someone opened the door and said: 'Right – go!' This was it, this was really happening! They opened the door, there was a camera right in my face and there was someone holding out a microphone for me to take. The cameraman was walking backwards as I was walking forwards. My mind didn't quite know what to do – do I look directly at the camera? Or do I look away? It felt like I was looking down the barrel of a loaded gun. Just as I made a decision to not quite look at the camera, the camera span off in a different direction and for a split second I thought: 'Am I following the camera or have I got to go up the stairs? Erm, oh yes, right, I'll go up the stairs then...' Thankfully this was the right decision!

My major fear was still that I was going to trip up. 'Oh God, this is like an obstacle course for someone with jelly legs,' which is what I had at that point as I gingerly moved Bambi-like down the steps and over the grille with the holes in it. My mantra on repeat at this point was still 'Please don't fall, please don't fall'. I was petrified that at any minute now I was going to slip arse over tit and make a complete idiot of myself.

I was used to going up on stage and I tried to tell myself this time was no different, but I was lying to myself and failing miserably. This was completely off the scale and I knew it.

As I stepped out, it wasn't the audience or the vastness that hit me; it was the silence. All I could hear was the sound of my heels clip-clopping down the stage. Otherwise there was just an eerie stillness spread across that huge space. I knew the audience had been told to stay silent but it was still the weirdest feeling. I couldn't really see all of them because of the bright lights, but I could feel their eyes bearing down on me, hundreds of people watching my every move. I was also aware of the tension in the studio, not just my own, but that of the audience's – could I sing or couldn't I? Would I make a mistake? Would I be any good?

It was then my eyes locked on the backs of those big red chairs. They looked so intimidating, and with a shock I became acutely aware that Jessie J, Tom Jones, Danny O'Donoghue and will.i.am were all sitting there, waiting patiently, and wanting me to impress them. I can honestly say, at that moment in time, I was the most nervous I have ever been in my life.

You could have heard a pin drop, then after what felt like a lifetime, the music started and I began to sing. I could tell I sounded a bit quivery and I had no saliva left in my mouth. But by the second line the audience started cheering and clapping which made me feel better and raised my spirits.

Out of the corner of my eye I could see this teenage girl going crazy and I remember looking at her thinking, 'Wow! I haven't even started yet – have you been told to go mad at everyone?' As I went through the verse I tried to control my breathing because it starts off really low, but watching it back now I can really hear my nerves.

I was halfway through the song but no one had turned round and in my head I was having a mental battle with myself. 'This is what you do every day so what are you getting nervous for now? Don't let nerves ruin this moment!'

Then as soon as it kicked into the chorus, and I hit some bigger notes, I suddenly noticed Tom Jones and Danny O'Donoghue spin around in their chairs at exactly the same time. The audience went mad and all I could think was – this is crazy! I've done it! I really couldn't believe it was me standing there with Tom Jones beaming away in my direction and Danny doing his pouty 'duck-face' thing and nodding along. I don't know how I kept singing when all I wanted to do was jump up and down and celebrate.

Before I knew it, the song was over and now all four coaches were facing me and I was grinning in shock as they gave their feedback. Will said some really nice things, Jessie called my voice 'insane', which was such a compliment coming from her, and Danny in his double denim said as soon as I hit that high note in the chorus he was sold and then he mentioned the power of my voice. But he added, 'I think maybe you did go a bit too powerful at the end,' which I agreed with because I could have done it so much better. He'd spotted the nerves had got to me and I was pleased he sort of knew I wouldn't normally sing like that. He said he'd be honoured to work with me, which was just unbelievable.

Then I turned to Tom, who was looking very debonair and statesman-like in a black crew neck and suit. 'What would you like to do with me, Tom?' I asked, to which everyone started pissing themselves laughing. Oh. My. God. What the hell did I just say? We'd been told by a producer beforehand that we shouldn't stand there like a lemon on stage and that we should banter with the coaches and ask them why they wanted to work with us. But somehow that had translated in my garbled brain as a proposition to Tom Jones. What an idiot!

Luckily Tom seemed amused. 'I'm a married man so I can't answer that question,' he said, chuckling. To which I replied, 'Me too!' I wanted the world to swallow me up. I thought, 'You idiot, you can guarantee that's going to get shown on telly!'

Moving it on, Tom said he loved the timbre of my voice and that as the weeks went on he felt I'd be able to handle a wide variety of material and that's why he'd like to have me on his team. I was just really overwhelmed; I hadn't expected one person to turn around let alone two. I was torn between both of them so it was such a hard decision to make.

I didn't have time to ponder and had to listen to my instinct and do it quick. Something deep down told me Tom wanted me more than Danny, and I liked what he'd said, so that's why I went with him.

Later on Danny was lovely to me all the way through the series so maybe I got that wrong, but I just had to go with my gut. I think in the end it was down to the fact that Tom has got the big voice, so if anyone could help me he could, and I liked everything he'd said earlier. So I thought, 'Yep, being mentored by Tom Jones, that works for me!'

As I left the stage he gave me a big hug. It was so surreal to be hugging Tom Jones and I babbled in his ear: 'You're a legend!' Durr – like no one's ever said that to him before. Why couldn't I have thought of something a bit more original to say?

I was now officially in shock and was led by someone on the production team straight into the room where my family had been watching with Reggie. I walked in stunned and saw them all crying and looking as stunned as me. Rob gave me a kiss and I was lost for words. They were all a wreck and I just didn't know what to say. We must have looked like a right load of muppets.

I was buzzing at having got through and was proud and relieved at having managed to get both Danny and Tom to turn around. But there was still the professional in me who knew I could have sung it better and a tiny part of me was a bit annoyed at myself.

In the car on the way home Mum kept asking me, 'Can I ring your brother? Can I ring your nan?' She wanted to tell everyone: my aunts, my uncles, my neighbours, my neighbour's cousin! We were all completely knackered and none of us could quite believe what had just occurred. By telling people it was as if we were reminding ourselves it was really happening.

Mum was so excited and wanted me to speak to everyone on the phone, but I'd reached a point where I couldn't talk any more. We'd been up since the crack of dawn and I was emotionally and physically drained. As I watched the cars flash by us as we made our way out of London, I still couldn't process what had just happened and was already thinking about what was going to happen in the next round. This was turning into a crazy ride – and while I was scared, I was gripping on tightly because I didn't want it to end just yet...

Chapter 7

Ready For Battle

Back at Potters someone had let slip what I was up to and by the time I got into work the next day the whole team knew I'd been auditioning – then they totally lost their marbles when, during our pre-show meeting, I told them I'd got through! Thankfully my bosses were brilliant about me taking all the time off I needed to give this opportunity my best shot.

The next round was called the Battles, where two people from each team would sing a duet together and then their coach would decide who would go through to the live stages. The rehearsals were scheduled for the second week of February and I headed down to London the day before to meet Faye to choose my outfit for the rehearsals, and to talk about what I'd wear for the actual Battle itself. In the evening all of us on Team Tom had been invited to the

Hospital Club (a swish bar in Covent Garden) for a night out with the man himself and it would also be the first time we'd all properly meet each other. A night out with Tom Jones? This was getting more surreal by the minute!

It didn't start well as I couldn't find the building and I was very nearly late. I had my iPhone Google map open and was walking up and down Endell Street in Covent Garden stressing out and thinking, 'It should be right here, but I can't see it.' Then it dawned on me it was one of those posh members' clubs that doesn't have a sign or even look like a bar. You just need the inside knowledge to know it's there.

So after finally locating the door and pressing the bell I was led through a minimalist black hallway up to this little room that was all done out like a French boudoir. Most of the other singers were already there.

The first person I got talking to was Sam Buttery and we just clicked straight away. He was lovely and we both ended up having a fit of the giggles because we were very much of the same mindset – thinking how on earth had we ended up in this bizarre but brilliant situation?

Also on Team Tom was Aundrea Nyle who was as bubbly as ever, and Barbara Bryceland who was a really glamorous Scot and acted like everybody's mum and was up for a good time. I met Lindsey Butler who was a real chatterbox and then I saw the big beardy bloke and his partner who had grabbed my attention at the Blinds. Matt and Sueleen were both truly lovely – Sueleen was also very motherly and was always concerned for other people, which is a really nice trait. Ruth Brown was there with her big bobble hat on – she was quite withdrawn. She'd just suffered a bereavement and I remember asking her a couple of times if she was OK.

Then there was a laid-back redhead called Denise Morgan, Adam Isaac who was a tall chiselled rocker with a great dry sense of humour, and then smiley Deniece Pearson who'd been in the eighties band Five Star and looked so starry with her rhinestoned shoulder pads, gloves and, well, rhinestoned everything really. They were all so friendly which was a relief and the production team often said to us that we were the friendliest team of them all – not that we like to brag about it!

So we were sat there around this low table making chit-chat but I think we all had one eye on the door because we knew that any moment Tom Jones was about to walk into this tiny room and into our lives. It was a free bar and everyone, myself included, had that dilemma – do I drink or do I not drink? And I was like: 'No, you drink!' But just a couple. Sam and I, like naughty schoolkids, went and helped ourselves to a small glass of wine each, because I needed something to steady my nerves before Tom came in.

I was sitting on a sofa next to Sam and there was lots of nervous giggling between us as we waited for the legend to arrive. Finally the door swung open and there was Sir Tom Jones himself, looking smart in a grey suit and with a big grin on his face. 'Hello Team!' he said, looking around at us all and we gave him a big cheer as he came in, followed by his management team. Sam and I looked at each other – this was bonkers!

By this point the only seat left when Tom joined us was a low pouffe in the middle of the group, so he just squatted down and had to perch on that. So there was the legend that is Tom Jones practically sat on the floor, while we were all sat on normal-sized chairs and sofas staring at him and in total awe of his presence. I don't think I can quite remember a word he said; all I thought was, 'Just wait until I tell everyone at home about this...'

He made a little speech along the lines of 'I'm really proud of my team' and then a waiter asked him what he wanted to drink. 'I want some champagne, of course!' he said with a glint in his eye, which made us all laugh. This definitely helped seal the deal – I thought he was amazing before and now I knew he was.

Then came the worst part of the evening – we had to sit there and watch each other's blind auditions on a big TV screen that was attached to the wall. I thought, 'Oh God, we've got to sit through this to see what our competition is like,' because I didn't know half of them until then. And worse than that, I'd got to sit there while everyone watched mine – I was already cringing and we hadn't even started yet.

First up was Aundrea. She was really good but as I watched her performance of Gnarls Barkley's 'Crazy' I could see she'd been nervous too, you could hear it in her voice. So it made me feel a bit less panicked when I realised I wasn't going to be the only one whose nerves had played a part in their performance.

Then it was my turn and I was terrified of how it was going to sound because I didn't like the way I'd sung some of it. A couple of the high notes I hadn't been comfortable with, so I was dreading how it was going to sound on telly and worried it would all just be a distorted mess. That was the worst-case scenario going through my head.

When I appeared on screen I was literally trying to hide myself inside the sofa – I pulled a cushion in front of my face and peeked at the telly from behind it. In the end it wasn't great, but not as completely terrible as I'd been imagining in my head. And because when I was doing the big notes they were all cheering, as we did for everyone's performance, I didn't hear half of it anyway.

It was actually a really emotional moment, which took me by surprise. As I watched myself on screen from behind that cushion it was then I had the realisation of

'Look what you've just done'. That's when it clicked and I thought, 'Oh my God, you did that. You got out of your comfort zone, you put yourself out there and look what you've achieved!'

Everyone was good and a potential contender, and it was then I began wondering who they were going to put me up against in the Battles. My first thought was Barbara Bryceland. She'd sung a beautiful rendition of 'Wild Horses', which Tom had clearly loved and I'd loved her audition too. I thought, 'I bet I'm gonna be up against her,' because she was like an older version of me with her powerful voice. Although they weren't quite the same, we both had big voices. I thought it was either going to be her or Ruth Brown, because again we were vocally quite similar. But to be honest, I didn't know which way it was going to go.

After that everyone started mingling and a lot of people made a beeline for Tom and swarmed around him. One of the producers kept nudging me to go and talk to him, but I couldn't. I was just rooted to the spot. Like when I'd been a little girl, my shyness was holding me back and stopping me from even saying hello to this fantastic man. Anyway, what on earth would someone like me have to say to someone like him? 'Oh, hi, Tom. Erm, do you know you're a legend? Oh yes, I told you that before, didn't I...?'

I just couldn't. Instead I wanted to stand and stare at

him from the other side of the room and try and remember every detail of this moment. Here I was in the same room as Tom Jones, someone I'd grown up listening to. For years at Potters we'd been doing a Tom Jones and Shirley Bassey medley. My good friend Siôn Hathway would be Tom and I'd do Shirley and we used to sing 'Baby It's Cold Outside' in another show as well. I stood there watching Tom chatting away to Matt and Sueleen and all I could think was, 'God, when you think of all the songs that he's done, anything with his voice on just makes the song. The word legend is bandied about a lot – but this guy actually is one.'

Tom seemed to be having a great time getting to know everyone, but we all had an early start the next day and I remember Mark, his son, who is also his manager, saying: 'OK, Tom, we've got to go now.' You could see his face drop. 'Oh no! Do I have to?' You could tell he would have been up for partying all night and they literally had to drag him away from us. To have his energy and enthusiasm for life is an inspiration and a wonderful thing to be around.

The next morning we had to be there at eight o'clock 'camera-ready' in the outfit that we'd chosen. The building where the Battle rehearsals were being filmed was a disused warehouse down a dead-end street in the London Bridge area. The warehouse had several levels and one floor was filled with a big white grand piano and a selection of funky furniture – retro black armchairs, spotlights and big silver mirrors. It looked like some kind of stylish New York loft apartment crossed with the set of *Dragons' Den*.

But while it looked like urban city glamour, it felt like outer Siberia! It was one of the coldest days of the winter and even inside you could see your own breath in the air. There was no central heating and we spent most of the time either huddled around one of the temporary heaters, rubbing our hands together wearing our coats, or outside on the even colder catering bus, which was basically a tatty old double decker where we spent most of the day in between filming and where we ate all our meals.

After a few make-up touch-ups we were taken upstairs and told to stand in a line – we were about to find out what we'd be singing and who we'd be singing it with. I was thinking, 'What am I going to be given and how am I going to cover it up if I hate the song?' When Tom came in we all clapped and cheered him and then we were paired up. As the duos got whittled down it got to the point where there were only Barbara, Adam, Denise Morgan and me left. So it was like – well, this one's pretty obvious, isn't it?

As I'd expected Barbara and I were both asked to step forward and I remember thinking, 'Bloody hell, she's gonna take some beating!' Tom said we both had very powerful voices and felt we were evenly matched. He then revealed the song we were going to be singing was Lady

Gaga's 'Edge Of Glory'. I didn't know it very well at all but Barbara was thrilled to bits and punched the air because she sang it at her gigs. So my first reaction was: 'Uh oh! I'm in big trouble here – she knows the song and I don't...'

During the next break in filming Barbara and I agreed we wanted to make it a really good duet. It's funny because we kept being told to talk like we were having a battle; after all, we were opponents. But I didn't want to look at it like that, I just wanted to enjoy it and give it my best shot.

However, I also knew I had to up my game. I'd only met her a couple of times but I could see Barbara had such a big personality and she wasn't afraid of talking to Tom and having a bit of a flirt in front of the camera. So I had to keep reminding myself to try and talk and not just to stand there like a lemon. Or gooseberry, should I say! I also believed that because she was so bubbly and outgoing and had such a great voice, she'd already got this in the bag. I could see Tom really liked her too, so my only real way forward in the Battle was just to try and sing my absolute best. There was nothing else I could do. If my singing wasn't good enough, then so be it.

Almost immediately we had a filmed session around the piano with Tom and the lyric sheet. The song had already been broken down so we could see who would sing which lines. I was in a bit of a panic, thinking, 'I don't know how the tune goes, I only know the chorus. And I've got to sing it right now?'

Because Barbara knew it, straight away she was properly going for it. 'Oh God, you need to learn this song – and quick!' I thought to myself. Luckily Tom seemed happy with how it was going but because Barbara was so comfortable with every aspect of the song, I could see we were on an uneven keel as a starting point.

I was quite lucky because Sunday was everybody's day off so I could do some serious catch-up at home on my own. I'd been really ill with a throat infection and was only just getting over it, so when we were working with Tom by the piano I couldn't belt it out as I would have liked because there wasn't any strength there. I was on antibiotics but I was trying to hide it because I didn't want anybody to know and I didn't want to make a fuss.

What I really needed to do was rest my voice, so I spent the next day going through what I wanted to do with my bits in the song. I didn't sing out or anything because I wanted to rest my vocal cords, but I just learnt it and got my head around it. By the end of the day I was like, 'Right, now you know what you're doing!'

Back in London the next day, my voice sounded a bit better and thank goodness it did, because even when we were having a warm-up together, Barbara and I were competing to sing the highest. It was all in jest, but hard as it is, and as much as you like each other, at a certain point you know you are in direct competition for your survival with that person and no one else.

This time our vocal session was with Tom and Cerys Matthews from Catatonia – she was smiley, down to earth and full of good advice. Cerys and Tom had duetted together on 'Baby It's Cold Outside' and through their easy manner together you could tell they were good mates. She kept making me laugh and at one point she turned to me and grinned, 'You've got a fair set of lungs on you!' I didn't really know what to say to that so I just mumbled, 'I try...' Another idiot moment!

So we started singing again and this time Barbara had got even louder. I thought if I do it at that volume as well it's just going to sound like a scream-off rather than a singing match, so I tried to hold back a bit. But obviously you can't really do that on a dancey pop song like 'Edge Of Glory', and by the time we got to the chorus you could probably hear the pair of us right down on the platform of London Bridge tube station, maybe even in the tunnels!

Cerys was killing herself laughing, saying, 'I've never heard such loud voices as you guys!' The final time we sang it we were halfway through the chorus when she came and stood right in the middle of me and Barbara, so we were both practically singing into her ears. She just stood there, flashed one of her big smiles and went, 'I just wanted to know what that would feel like.'

Between filming we had to wait upstairs on the catering bus (it was supposedly warmer on the upper level) and they gave us blankets to wrap around ourselves because it was so unbelievably cold in there. I was just praying the chill wasn't going to start affecting my voice. As I was beginning to realise, filming a TV show involved a lot of hanging around, but luckily Barbara had her iPad with Trivial Pursuit on it so we all played. Not that I'm very good at Trivial Pursuit – I can only answer the pink showbiz questions – but it was a good way for us to pass the time and obviously very rock 'n' roll!

The Battles were recorded the following week at the Fountain Studios in Wembley on a new, bigger, boxing-ring-style set. As we had our final run-through in the studio and as I took in the even bigger rows of audience seating, I decided on a plan of action. This time around I was determined to enjoy it and gave myself a pep talk: 'Don't get yourself in a state like you did at the Blinds because you won't sing it as well as you know you can.' I knew it would be nerve-wracking, of course, but I had to make sure of two things: one, the nerves didn't spoil my voice and two, the nerves didn't spoil the moment.

I did end up feeling a lot calmer that day, maybe in a way because I was so convinced that Barbara was going to get through. As far as I was concerned Barbara had the personality and the voice and Tom was going to pick her. Meanwhile I felt like I wasn't on anybody's radar and couldn't compete with someone as bubbly as Barbara.

In a way, thinking she had it sewn up took my primary focus back on to the song. My main motivation was that I just wanted us to sound good together. All the way through the rehearsals I was like, 'We don't want to get too loud so that it sounds as if we're trying to overpower each other,' and we both kind of agreed on that. But I knew as soon as we got out there Barbara would just go hell for leather, so I kept reminding myself not to over-sing and keep in control, because this is a song where you really need control.

Backstage Barbara was all dolled up in this red cocktail dress with her big glamorous blonde bombshell hair and there was me in a black skater dress with my hair pulled back in a side plait. She looked like she was off to a fabulous party, but I didn't mind because I actually really liked what I was wearing and this time I was determined to be myself out there and be the best I could. I took a deep breath and waited for Holly to introduce us. 'Entering the ring, two ladies with many differences but one thing in common: voices that will make your TV shake ... it's the battle of the belters!'

As Barbara was announced I could feel the adrenaline buzzing through my veins. This was nerves, yes, but in a different way to last time. Barbara punched the air and practically ran on to the set. You've gotta love her! Then it was my turn to come on from the other side, so I stepped up, smiled and gave the crowd a big wave. It was weird at first because obviously this time all the coaches were staring at us right from the beginning, but before I knew it the music had started and once it was my turn to sing I started to enjoy myself.

The audience were clapping along and seemed to be loving it, Tom was grinning away like a Cheshire cat, and Jessie was dancing in her seat, which caught my eye. She saw me and smiled back, which I was pleased about because I'd tried to make eye contact with each of them to try and make them watch me.

Now was not the time to be a wallflower in the background and here I was actually relishing my time in the limelight. Meanwhile Will's eyes looked like they were about to pop out of his head at Barbara's vocals and Danny was dancing along and mouthing 'wow'. My voice held out, I felt myself feed off the energy of the audience and I really was loving every second, feeling every note and having the time of my life up there.

All too soon it was over. All four coaches jumped to their feet and the whole crowd gave us a standing ovation, which seemed to go on forever. To me it felt a lot better than the Blinds – more comfortable, like I'd actually performed and

I wasn't just standing there like an idiot rooted to the spot with fear for the whole performance. I felt we'd done what we set out to do, which was a really good duet. I looked at Barbara – I don't think either of us could believe the reaction from the audience and we were both exhilarated by it. This was something we'd never expected.

But then it went quiet again. Now it was time to get down to the serious bit. One of us had to go home and I'd just had such a ball on the stage, the fighter in me emerged and I knew I didn't want it to be me. Before I would have said I'd had a great time and done my best, so no regrets. But now I cared, now I desperately wanted to stay. I knew it was in me to give a performance like that again, and I wanted to do so very much.

It was down to Tom to make that decision. I glanced over at him and he was now looking grave. You could see it in his eyes, he was genuinely thinking, 'Who do I pick?' Holly walked over and I looked up at her thinking, 'Bloody hell, you're tall and I've got heels on.' Oh, and in case anyone's wondering, yes, she really is that beautiful up close! She stood between us while each coach gave us their feedback.

Danny said Barbara brought the house down, but if he had to pick he'd take me through to the next round, then Will said he'd got a crush on Barbara which was a really funny moment, but he never actually said which one of us he would pick. Next Jessie J went into some detail about the technical side of our singing and said I had a crazy confidence with my technique – so I was glad I'd come across as vaguely confident this time.

Then it was Tom's turn and he looked very pensive and really torn. I wondered whether all along he'd thought Barbara and then maybe I'd just done something that made him rethink. I don't know, but he certainly looked like he was having this massive dilemma. Maybe he was regretting putting us both together, who knows? I thought we'd both given a performance that should merit both of us staying, but of course that wasn't possible.

Time was ticking and Tom still hadn't given his answer. Holly chipped in. 'Tom, it is time to make your decision. Who is the winner of this Battle?'

'This is maybe the hardest thing that I have ever done.' He frowned, pausing for a moment, rubbing his face as he thought out loud. 'They are both as strong as each other...' There was another pause while he gathered his thoughts.

Tom spoke again. He'd made his decision. 'It's hard but I think the one that should go through to the live shows is ... Leanne!'

What? I was totally shocked. Then Holly grabbed my hand and flung it up like I'd just won a boxing match. I hugged Barbara straight away because I felt really bad for her and I told her she didn't deserve to be out now. And I genuinely felt that if we could both have gone through we should have done.

I think that little pep talk I'd given myself earlier had really worked because when I finally saw it on TV, after we'd left the stage Jessie mentioned to Tom that if she'd had to pick one of us she would have gone with me because I showed more light and shade. The key to getting through that round had been not to over-sing but to try and stay in control.

I walked off stage through the audience and again was whisked straight to where my friends and family were watching. This time there were seven of them and when I opened the door they all went ballistic. My parents were there sobbing away, and everyone was jumping up and down and had tears streaming down their faces – as they ran towards me I just couldn't take any of it in.

One thing that made me laugh was that despite the madness of the situation I looked at Rob and the first thing I thought was, 'What the hell are you wearing, Rob?' He had some kind of beige slouchy jumper on. I was thinking, 'For God's sake, why didn't you put a shirt on? This is what happens when I don't dress you!' It's funny because my mum said to me afterwards, 'I could tell that was the first thing you thought!'

Bless him, though, because he came forward to give me a kiss and as he did I stepped forward at the same time, so we had this really awkward moment where he ended up kissing my shoulder instead of my cheek, which was hilarious. That ended up on telly too so everyone took the mickey out of him about that one for weeks afterwards.

I was still on an adrenaline rush. It was all so hard to process and I couldn't take in the fact I'd just got through to the live rounds. We all had a drink in the cafe bar at the Fountain Studios to calm ourselves down, but the high was a mixed emotion because you were also in there with all the people who hadn't got through. While some singers were being crazy happy about it, they were sat next to the person who hadn't succeeded. So I tried to contain myself a bit and think about how they were feeling, because they must have been gutted and I didn't want to rub anyone's faces in it. I saw Barbara over the other side of the room and tentatively went over and met her family. They were all so lovely and she reassured me she'd had a ball and there were no hard feelings and we said goodbye with another big hug.

It was over a month until the series was going out on telly and we were instructed to keep our participation a secret and only to tell close friends and family that we were on the show. I was too scared to tell people in any case and I didn't dare tell anyone because I didn't want to get into trouble with the production team, so I just kept it to a select few.

At that point we didn't have a clue how big the show was going to be and then slowly but surely the publicity machine started to crank up and people gradually became aware of it. I remember one time I'd been watching *EastEnders* on BBC1 when suddenly a promo for *The Voice* came on and I saw my face flash up for literally a millisecond. I called to Rob to come and see – this was all getting scarily real! There were interviews with the coaches in the papers and in all the celebrity magazines and so much speculation about the show. Soon it was all anyone was talking about – everywhere I turned there seemed to be something on *The Voice*.

There were four episodes of the blind auditions and I found out the day before the series started that mine wasn't on until the third programme. So Rob and I went round to my parents' house to see all the episodes, as they wanted us to be together.

Watching that first episode I felt really jittery – I don't know why because I wasn't even in it. It started with an explanation of the format and the coaches and then suddenly the faces of some of the people who'd auditioned flashed on to the screen and – blink and you'd miss me – there I was again, and everyone in the room started screaming as if I'd already won the bloody thing!

I still didn't know a lot of the other singers so it was good to see who else was on the show. Of all the auditions,

I thought Joelle Moses came over really well and Bo Bruce's version of 'Without You' was great, something really different. Ruth Brown had a fantastic audition and she'd been getting a lot of press attention because Tom had mentioned in interviews he had a potential winner in his team. I'd seen a few things in which he talked about this great girl he'd got in his group who was a gospel singer and I was like, 'Oh well, that ain't me then!'

I really liked Becky Hill's voice as well, but I remember thinking Jaz Ellington had an amazing tone and like a lot of people I was convinced he was going to win it, because his voice was definitely something special. But what also went through my mind, which I think a lot of other people thought too, was they've shown him doing two songs on telly. First he sang 'The A Team' and then a spur-of-the-moment version of 'Ordinary People', which left will.i.am in floods of tears. He'd been given two chances to show what he could do and had blown everyone away in the process, so I kind of thought, well, he's got this in the bag then!

Two weeks later a big crowd of family and friends gathered to watch my episode: my mum, my dad, my brother Daniel, his fiancée Carly, my nephew Ben, Auntie Netty, Uncle Martin, my cousin Danielle, Mel, Darren and Rob. About twelve of us all squeezed around the telly in my parents' front room. There were drinks and nibbles everywhere – Mum had done 'tea on the table' (a favourite of mine!) – and everyone was in the mood for a party.

As a well-done present my parents had bought me an iPad, because we'd been told by the production team to tweet when we were watching to help generate interest in the show and our performances. That morning Dad said, 'I'm picking you up at some point in the day.' I asked what for and he replied: 'I'm just taking you out if that's OK!' So despite not really being able to afford it he bought me an iPad as a surprise. In the shop I said, 'You really don't have to do this,' but he explained that I needed one to do all of my tweeting. And I could see he really wanted to treat me so that was very sweet.

As the episode started there was a big part of me that just wanted to hurry home and sit on our couch, watch it just with Rob and leave them to their party. But I knew how much it meant to my parents for us to be together, so I just got myself a large glass of wine and sat there with that. Obviously I'd seen my audition once before behind a cushion on the night we met Tom, but I hadn't seen the footage of what the coaches said and the interviews with my family beforehand and afterwards.

Meanwhile everyone else was hysterical and when I appeared on the screen they all roared. 'God, this is actually being beamed out, this is on national television – how bizarre is that?' I thought to myself. There was Mum and Dad and Rob and me walking on the red carpet and being interviewed and then there I was silently walking down the steps on to the stage, trying not to trip up in those massive heeled shoes.

As I began to sing 'If I Were A Boy', everyone in the room had tears in their eyes and soppy smiles on their faces, whereas all I could do was frown at the screen and think, 'God, you sound like a bag of nerves.' Of course then my parents wanted to rewind it and watch it about 500 times afterwards. For me, watching it brought back so many strong emotions that I had felt on the day, and I was pleased and relieved to see that what had been televised was a fair representation of what had actually happened at the audition.

What really struck me watching the Blinds, and what I really liked, was the fact that nobody had been humiliated. The reason why people weren't getting put through was because they weren't quite the coaches' cup of tea. They were all hugely talented and not a single singer was made to look bad. I was relieved to know I was a part of a show that wasn't into belittling people, or making them look stupid or feel rotten if they weren't picked. There was still an air of positivity about everything and it just felt like a celebration of good singing.

When my episode finished I switched on my iPad and my mobile and there were hundreds of emails, mainly Twitter message alerts, and I was dreading looking through them all. What if I got completely annihilated on Twitter, how was I going to cope with that?

But the reaction was really good. I don't think I got anything bad through which was such a relief, just thousands of upbeat messages from people who'd seen the show. It felt so weird – obviously I was used to getting feedback at gigs, but this was from all over the country. People I'd never even met before.

Finally I could relax and let my hair down. We spent the rest of the evening having a little party and it got quite merry, then Rob and I went to a local bar in Oulton Broad to meet some friends from Potters after their show. It was wicked to see everyone, they were so pleased for me, but I soon started to feel so knackered. I think all the stress and anxiety of the day had finally caught up with me and also in the back of my mind, in true Leanne style, I couldn't totally let go and enjoy the moment, because I was already starting to worry about what was coming next. In two weeks' time I was moving to London...

Chapter 8

Going Live

My battle was televised on the Sunday I moved to London to begin rehearsals for the live shows and because I'd felt better about this one I was actually looking forward to seeing it. I'd really enjoyed the performance and unlike the blind audition I hadn't sounded like a complete bag of nerves. By now *The Voice* had become incredibly popular, the reaction from people I met was mental and I was so pleased to just be a small part of it.

As ever I read the instructions email over and over again to make sure I hadn't missed anything important: 'The date with your coach is 16 April. This is where you will get your song and work around the piano with your coach. The rest of the dates will follow. For the rehearsal you will need to wear an unbranded outfit. This includes T-shirts with logos, brands or cartoon characters. Please avoid stripes. We don't expect you to go shopping for a full new wardrobe. Just piece together outfits you would wear in your everyday life, but make sure they're TV worthy.'

This ended up costing me a bloody fortune. I flicked through the hangers in my wardrobe and just thought, 'Well, I can't wear any of that.' So I headed out to the shops to find some bits to make myself look vaguely presentable. We'd been advised to pack enough clothes for six weeks but I remember thinking, 'I ain't gonna be there for that long!'

All the singers who didn't live in London were to share accommodation in Barnet, north London, which was near the Elstree Studios in Hertfordshire where the live shows were being filmed. When I arrived at the block of flats I was informed I'd be sharing mine with Becky Hill who was on Jessie J's team. I hadn't met Becky during any of the rehearsals or filming – all I'd really seen of her was her blind audition on the telly. I thought she had a great voice with an amazing husky tone. However, she was only eighteen years old, and I don't know whether this had been down to the editing, but she seemed to have a whole 'stroppy teen' thing going on. Being ten years older, I presumed we'd been teamed up so I'd keep her under control and I was wondering how the hell we were going to get along in a small flat together.

I was preparing myself for the babysitter role, but as soon as Becky turned up with her mum and dad I could see immediately that she wasn't how she'd come across on TV. She was bright, full of energy and had a really wise head on her shoulders for someone so young. There may have been a ten-year age gap between us, but we clicked straight away and became really close as the weeks went on. And to be honest, she was the one who worked out how to use the washing machine, the dishwasher, the oven – in fact she looked after me half the time!

It turned out Sam Buttery was in the flat next door to us, which was brilliant. Sam being Sam went straight to Tesco and bought some snacks and wine, and we got together in our flat to watch the Battles being broadcast.

All the contestants who were staying in the flats ended up cramming into ours that night. Everyone was so excited and nervous, and the TV was getting louder and louder as we all screamed like a load of overexcited nut-jobs every time one of us appeared on screen. I texted Barbara Bryceland when it was our turn, but I could barely hear what we sounded like thanks to all the noise in the room. I didn't care though, it was brilliant to be able to watch it with the others, knowing we'd all got through and we all had this mad musical journey ahead of us.

Personally, I've always been a real homebody and I dread being away from it for too long. But because everyone in the flats was in the same boat, there was a great connection between us. We looked out for each other and the more time we spent together, the more it really did start to feel like a bit of a *Voice* family.

The next morning we began rehearsals for the first live show which would be broadcast the following Saturday. There were only five of us left in each team and none of us wanted to be the first to go. In Team Tom there was the lovely and quirky Matt and Sueleen, Sam Buttery who had so much personality and a great voice, Adam Isaac who was such a confident musician and singer, and the talented Ruth Brown, who I think Tom had a soft spot for. And then there was me.

We'd been asked to send through a list of songs we'd be happy to sing in the live rounds, so I'd carefully selected mine and included all my favourite big diva ballads. But when I found out what they had actually chosen for me to sing at first I thought I'd misheard. Or they'd muddled up my song choice with someone else's. Nope, I'd heard it right the first time.

Out of all the songs that Tom could have suggested for me, this was something that had never been and never would be on any of my lists – it was 'Who Knew' by Pink. Don't get me wrong, I love Pink and have been to see her in concert – she was brilliant – but I have never thought her songs suited me! So to be presented with this song – completely out of my comfort zone – on the first live show was rather daunting. I felt disappointed and all the excitement I'd been feeling kind of evaporated there and then.

But I took a deep breath and decided to go with it. It wasn't the kind of song I'd ever choose to sing in a million years, but I've always been open to new stuff so I just thought, 'Let's give it a go.' Plus it was the first week of the live shows and I didn't want anybody to think that I was being disrespectful or rude. Maybe other people wouldn't have given a monkey's about things like that and would've put their foot down, but I was really aware of not wanting to come across as a diva.

I went in to rehearse around the piano with Tom and straight away he asked me how I felt about the song. 'It's, erm, really different,' I mumbled, trying to be diplomatic. 'I'm not sure really, but I'll try it.' I'd never sung 'Who Knew' before in my life and while they seemed pretty pleased with my initial attempts, I wasn't happy, I really wasn't happy at all. This was the first time the public would be voting on my performance – these ninety seconds would decide my whole future on the show – yet I felt that I wouldn't be able to demonstrate what I could do.

It was the one and only day I felt like that. You don't realise how much pressure you're putting yourself under and I suppose at some point something's got to give. When I rang my parents at home later that evening, I just brushed it off and said, 'Yeah, I was a bit pissed off, but it's fine.' I felt a hell of a lot worse than I actually admitted, but I wasn't going to worry anyone else with my own crap.

I came out of that rehearsal feeling really despondent and me being me I kept it all to myself, hiding my disappointment beneath a fixed smile. I tried to look on the bright side, but when I heard the great songs everyone else had lined up, and that other people had been allowed to change their choices, I started to feel even worse.

I was in the make-up room getting ready to film a pre-recorded interview when Yvie popped in and asked how I was feeling about the song. I think she knew and probably agreed that this was the wrong choice for me. But because I didn't want to cause any aggro by saying I hated it and didn't want to be that person who never seems happy with what they're given, I tried to say it was fine.

The only problem was, me being a bit of a sap, I said it to her as my eyes were welling up with tears. What an idiot! But I couldn't help it; the truth was I was gutted. I guess that might sound a bit drippy to anyone else, but to me, to give me a song so far away from the type of singer I am was a kick in the teeth.

Yvie could obviously see how I was really feeling and was as supportive as ever. She disappeared and came back five minutes later with a producer, who came in, sat down next to me and tried to convince me that I'd sounded amazing in rehearsal. She explained the reason this song had been suggested was they wanted to challenge me, which to be honest got my back up even more because they don't know what you've done in your life, so they really hadn't got a clue what was challenging you and what wasn't. I wanted to say to her, 'I've sung just about every single genre possible from opera to rock and I know what works for me – I've spent the last twenty-eight years working that out. I've challenged myself my whole life and now, in front of millions of people and on live TV, is not the time to challenge myself again!' But at the same time you think, 'Well, maybe they can hear something that I can't,' so I just sat there and tried to latch on to her point of view.

I knew if I had to I would just try and do the best I could with the song, but I also wanted the chance to sing something that showcased my voice – I hadn't done that on the show yet. I was too nervous when I sang 'If I Were A Boy', and 'Edge Of Glory' was a great pop song but that had been a duet and I'd had to share the big notes. In the end I was given the opportunity to sing another song for Tom and I chose 'Hurt' by Christina Aguilera. I thought I was going in there off-camera to show just him, but no, I got there and all the cameras and crew were ready. Obviously I had forgotten the part about it being a TV show and that they'd want to capture every little hiccup!

By now I was mortified about the whole situation that had been created. Thankfully Tom was understanding and patient, but because I hadn't had a chance to rehearse the song with Pete the piano player (who'd literally had about three seconds to learn it), we came in at different parts. So all in all it was getting more horrendous by the minute...

When it finally ground to a halt Tom thought about it for a moment and said: 'Yeah, it was great but you sounded very similar to Christina Aguilera. With the Pink song I think you bring something different to it.' There I was stood in front of Tom Jones, a legend who has been in this industry for years and he's saying you sound great singing this song, and meanwhile everyone else was looking at me (and probably their watches) expectantly – I had to make a decision. So I took a deep breath and said, 'OK, shall we just forget this ever happened?' and luckily everybody laughed so I didn't feel like a total idiot. Then they all started swarming around me telling me how well they thought I'd sung 'Who Knew' and by that point I just wanted the world to swallow me up.

I'm glad I tried to fight my corner but as someone who hates making a fuss, the stress and the pressure had felt horrendous as a result. It was time to move on, dust myself down and give this song my best shot. It's funny thinking back to that day now because it was the one time I let the pressure of being on *The Voice* get to me.

On the day of the actual live show I managed to get myself into a more positive mindset about the whole thing, but then the producers decided they wanted to change my outfit because the one planned just wasn't working with the song. So at the last minute I was zipped into a black dress with white curves down it. I thought I looked OK with my hair and make-up, but when I watched it back somehow I'd ended up with bouffed-up middle-aged-lady hair and was dressed like I was going to a wedding. I just didn't look comfortable. And that was the first time I realised HOW different you can look and come across on telly than in real life if you're not careful!

Even at the time I remember catching myself in the mirror and thinking, 'You don't look like you today. You're singing a song that isn't you and you're in a dress that you'd never ever normally wear. But sod it, go with it and do your best!'

The icing on the cake was when I found out I would be following Jaz Ellington who was singing that amazingly soulful ballad 'At Last'. He was one of the favourites on Will's team, and had a stylish grand piano on stage with him and lots of low fog swirling around his feet during his performance. I would have loved a song like 'At Last', but instead I had to come on dressed up to the nines, trying to do a Pink song I barely knew. As far as I was concerned my future on *The Voice* was looking shaky to say the least...

I stood by the side of the stage while Jaz performed and thought, 'Yep, you're screwed.' His standing ovation and the screams from the audience just confirmed it. 'How am I supposed to follow that?' But at the same time I knew I had to snap myself out of it and think positive – being part of this show was an amazing one-off experience that was never going to happen to me again in my life, and I was so lucky to be experiencing it. For however much longer I was going to be part of *The Voice,* I wanted to make sure I enjoyed every single second and gave it my all.

Once I got on stage my biggest fear was that I was going to forget the words because I really didn't know the song very well. Thankfully I managed to remember all of them. I tried to come across as if I liked the song, but again when I watch it back I can see how uncomfortable I look with everything from the song to my costume. And then to top it all off these cheesy contemporary dancers appeared and started twirling around next to me! That was so unexpected, it made me giggle!

I didn't feel myself on stage that night, but thankfully the feedback was good – Tom explained he'd wanted to take me out of my comfort zone with the song and that I'd now proved I could sing anything. Meanwhile Jessie admitted at first she wasn't sure about the song choice, but said I'd won her over because I didn't sing it like Pink. Their positive comments were all a huge relief and made me feel loads better, but I still knew I could do so much more than that.

After we went off air we had forty-five minutes to prepare for the pre-recorded results show that would go out the following night. The format was that the three singers with the highest public vote from Team Tom would automatically get to continue in the competition, but Tom would then have to choose one act to send home from the two lowest scorers.

I was fully expecting to still be standing there after the top three had been announced and when the music of doom started I felt my stomach lurch in full-on panic. Had I done enough to stay in the competition? After pausing for dramatic effect, Holly Willoughby began to announce the results. 'The first artist saved by the viewers votes is … Ruth Brown!' Well, that wasn't exactly a shocker. But I couldn't call what was going to happen next. Still standing there with our hearts in our mouths were Adam Isaac, Sam Buttery, Matt and Sueleen and me. Holly's voice boomed out again: 'The next artist saved by the viewers is … Adam Isaac!'

It felt like an eternity standing there. I was praying I'd get through, because in my head I desperately wanted a second chance to get this right. It had been a tough week and I wanted to prove myself. But all I could do now was cross my fingers and hope for the best…

'And the final artist saved by the viewers' votes is … Leanne Mitchell!' YES! When I heard my name I could have cried with relief. I felt like I'd got through by the skin of my teeth, but I'd been given my second chance and I was going to grab it with both hands!

My euphoria was quickly stemmed as my thoughts turned to the others. I waited by the side of the stage to see what was going to happen next – it was a toss-up between Sam and Matt and Sueleen. Tom looked torn and so was I;

we'd all bonded in such a short space of time and I didn't want either of them to go home. In the end Tom opted to save Matt and Sueleen and while I was delighted for them, I was gutted for Sam who got really upset, which choked me up even more.

As filming ended we had to do interviews whilst still on stage and the whole experience of the first vote-off was really emotional for all of us. It shows how close we'd become and I felt so sorry for Sam because I felt he hadn't been given much of a chance to show what he could do. It made me realise even more how important song choice was in this competition. Whatever song I was given in the next round I had to be happy with it, because I never wanted to face a scenario like this week ever again.

I wasn't kidding myself that I'd got through because I'd given the performance of my life. I felt I'd been lucky, to be honest, and it meant I wanted to make sure that in the next round I demonstrated who I really was. That was the point where I decided that I was going to stick to who I was in future and I wasn't going to let a TV show change me or make me come across like someone I'm not.

The following week no one on Team Tom was up for the public vote so we were able to just enjoy rehearsing our group number, which was Stevie Wonder's 'Higher Ground'. I was lucky because I got the first line, so I could play around with it and ad-lib during the intro, which felt great and was similar to the sort of thing I'd do with the singers at Potters. I really enjoyed it and, of course, the pressure was off.

I was still convinced I'd be out in the next round anyway, so I just wanted to have fun up there before I had to worry about competing again. It's funny because that week during 'Higher Ground' my friends said it was the first time they'd seen the real me on the show, the performer they all knew. You can see it in my face when you watch it back – I'm happy, I'm getting a kick out if it, I'm in my element. Unlike the week before!

So for the next live show I was raring to go. I knew I'd got through by the skin of my teeth and I was so grateful to still be in the competition. I was determined that this time I'd have more say in what I was singing and what I looked like up there. This time I just wanted to be 'me'.

The song that was suggested to me was 'I Put A Spell On You', which immediately excited me because I'd sung it before and it's a really good number to show off your voice. Another thing I liked about it was that while people knew the song, they didn't relate it to one specific singer. So you're not going to be directly compared to someone else, which was good – you could put your own stamp on it.

I felt much more comfortable in rehearsal because I knew the song, and after my experiences on the first live show I wanted it to just be about the music and the vocal. I didn't want to wear any big statement outfit, so I asked to be in black and have my hair up and off my face, and Faye had got me some lovely vintage jewellery to finish off the look. I didn't want to be judged on anything apart from the voice. I know you're on TV, so you're going to get criticised from all areas, but I knew I had to stay true to myself and remember why I'd entered in the first place. This was how I wanted to play it and I just wanted to stand there and sing.

That week I went back to Potters for a day as the production team wanted to film me there. While it was so lovely to see everyone, it felt really strange to be there with a camera crew. The producer asked me to sing in the show that evening and the most cringe-making moment was when they got Rob to sit at the front of the theatre as if I was singing directly to him from the stage. But as ever, I did as I was told, but drew the line when they kept asking me to declare my undying love for my husband for the cameras – sorry, but that's private and I'm not going to trot that one out on cue. I absolutely hate it when people use their relationships in situations like that. And needless to say, I've never sung to him in my life and I doubt he'd want me to either!

The funny thing is that particular day was in the middle of an off-season police-break, so the whole resort was filled with policemen and women. The producers wanted to film the guests watching me sing 'I Put A Spell On You', but most of them were undercover policemen so they couldn't be seen on camera! In the end I think a few of the wives agreed to be filmed, which was a relief and stopped the whole trip being a complete waste of time.

On the day of the live show we had to be on stage in full costume and make-up at stupid o'clock in the morning for a full run-through, which was also when the big bosses, the show's executive producers, see your performance for the final time and suggest any last-minute changes. Normally they sat at the back of the empty audience watching the rehearsal on a monitor (to see what it'll look like on telly). But this time, after I'd sung, one of them came running down to me to say how amazing she thought I was and how good the performance had been.

She seemed really excited and I had to stop myself from saying, 'Now can you see why I didn't want to sing that Pink song?' It wasn't that I agreed with her and thought I was amazing or anything, it was just the previous week I hadn't been singing the type of music that suited me.

At the time I remember thinking that was quite a big thing, to actually have someone get up from the back of the studio and come over and tell you they think you're quite good! So it gave me a bit of a confidence boost and I couldn't wait to get out there, show what I could do and, most of all, try and enjoy it. The whole set-up felt great that week and I loved how they'd arranged the stage. There was going to be a huge chandelier with all these ribbons hanging from it and the icing on the cake for me was that saxophonist

Nigel Hitchcock, who has toured with Tom and is a hugely respected musician, was going to be playing beside me.

That night as I performed it felt incredible. The studio audience seemed to be enjoying it and when I finished there was this huge roar and a standing ovation from all four coaches, which meant so much to me. It wasn't perfect but it felt so much better than anything else I'd done up until that point on the show. I'd felt confident and in control and I think that came through in my voice and in my performance. If that had been the previous week I wouldn't have minded going home on that performance, whereas if I'd gone on the back of the Pink song I would have had so many regrets.

The coaches all said they'd felt the confidence and the emotion in my delivery, which was great to hear, because that was exactly what I'd been trying to achieve. It was a huge relief that I'd managed to get that across and all I could think at that point was – phew!

When it came to the results, only the person with the highest public vote would automatically go through to the semi-final and I wasn't at all surprised to hear Ruth Brown's name called out as everyone was talking about her as a potential winner. Then it was between me, Adam Isaac and Matt and Sueleen. Only one of us could go through and again it was down to Tom to make that decision. As ever I didn't have a clue which way this was heading. Standing there as the whole studio crackled with tension, I just wanted to be put out of my misery.

When Tom said my name my hand swooped to my mouth – it felt incredible. This really was starting to feel like the biggest achievement of my life. I knew I wasn't the favourite, but to have got through to the semi-final meant more to me than I could put into words.

When I woke up the next day I still couldn't quite believe I was through to the semis – it was the best feeling in the world. In addition, Ruth and I had an easier week ahead of us because all we had to do was prepare a group number, which we could enjoy without being judged. As far as I was concerned Ruth was the favourite to win the whole thing, so I was determined to get the most out of my performances before I was voted off. Our song was Florence & The Machine's 'Shake It Out', which was a totally left-field choice, but it worked really well because we're both belty singers and it was great to be able to play around with the riffs and the ad-libs while the pressure was off.

Originally I was given the Aretha Franklin song 'I Never Loved A Man The Way I Love You' for the semi-final, which wasn't something I'd sung before but I could see where they were going as Tom had really liked 'I Put A Spell On You'. I was a bit worried that it was another old song because I didn't want to keep going down that route, but I liked it and thought it had lots of potential.

Then as I was working through the song with Tom at the piano rehearsal, his manager Mark came over and asked if we could stop for a second. 'I don't know if this is working...' he explained. 'It's not a big enough song for you and I think we can do better.' I was fine either way, as I enjoyed the song, but I could see his point. Then somebody said, 'Oh, we've got the music to "Run To You" here – do you want to try that one?' Erm, does a bear sh*t in the woods? I'd been suggesting 'Run To You' every week so I was more than happy with that suggestion.

Pete the pianist played it through a couple of times so I could get my head around the edited version, then as I sang it for the first time Tom started to get a bit choked up, which really took me by surprise. 'Bloody hell, this is a first...' I thought. 'Looks like this one's working then.'

It just felt so natural to be singing 'Run To You' because I've always loved the songs from *The Bodyguard* soundtrack – they are such big, powerful ballads and it was that kind of music that made me want to be a singer in the first place. As a kid the likes of Whitney Houston and Mariah Carey were who I would aspire to be. It was so weird to think that after all those years warbling along to the *Bodyguard* CD in my bedroom as a kid, now I really was going to be singing one of these songs on live TV. I still can't get my head around that now!

I felt like I bonded with Tom that week. We'd finished

rehearsing in front of the camera and the crew were packing away their equipment, but I decided to hang back with Pete and give 'Run To You' one last run-through. I'm sure Tom was due to be somewhere else, but he just picked a chair up, plonked it right in front of me, went 'Go on then!' and stayed to listen. I am sure he had a trillion other things he should have been doing, but it was sweet he took the time to cast his expert ear over my rendition for one last time.

Even though I was loving my new song choice, there was a part of me that was a teeny bit concerned people were going to compare my performance with Whitney's, and obviously no one wants to be compared to Whitney because whoever you are you're just going to pale in comparison. Plus there was the fact that she'd just died in such tragic circumstances and I didn't want anyone to think I was going for some kind of sympathy vote. So I spoke to them about tweaking it enough to make it my own, without ruining such a beautiful song.

As I've said before, as far as I was concerned, Ruth Brown had been the favourite from the start, and as a result I'd always felt a bit like the underdog that nobody had really noticed. Before the semis I'd go and have meetings in Tom's dressing room to discuss what we wanted to sing if I got to the final and I'd think, 'There's no way I'm going to be in the final so what are we talking about this for?' I wasn't trying to be negative, just realistic. So while song titles were being bandied about, I couldn't even allow myself to think that far ahead.

However, when it got to the semi-final stage and I was still there, clinging on, I think people started to notice me a bit more. But I wasn't going to kid myself – it was clear Ruth would be going through to the final for Team Tom; she'd got through on the public vote every single time and I hadn't. So I was just determined to enjoy myself and leave the show happy, having sung one of my favourite songs in the world.

In the end the semi-final became a really nostalgic day because I completely believed my journey was about to come to an end. All week I'd been joking with Becky Hill that this was our final and we may as well think of it as that, because we sure as hell weren't going to be there the next week for the real thing. As I went through the dress rehearsal, hair and make-up and my final warm-up sessions with Yvie, all I could think was, 'This is the last time I'm going to be doing this,' and it hit home all over again just how amazing this experience had been.

When the show began, the adrenaline was pumping through my every vein as I waited to be taken into the studio, but while I was excited about performing, I also felt a strange calmness. The pressure was off because ultimately I knew I was going home.

That night the special guest stars were pop princess Cheryl Cole and pop queen Kylie Minogue. Their sleek white Winnebagos were positioned side by side with their own sectioned-off outside areas, just opposite the stuffy, airless, temporary Portakabin otherwise known as 'The V Room', where we were held until it was our turn to perform.

I didn't get to meet Kylie because we were never in the same place at the same time, which was a shame. I could have bored her with my stories of doing 'The Loco-Motion' around the living room as a kid! But Becky and I got chatting to Cheryl Cole who was lovely. She was tiny too (and her mum was even tinier) and for someone so famous she seemed really down to earth. She gave us some hard-earned advice, telling us to make sure we really enjoyed the whole experience and warning that if we wanted to stay sane we should never search for ourselves online and should always ignore the negative crap that comes with being in the public eye. 'Not every day is a good day, but the good always outweighs the bad,' she added, sagely.

Then I was taken backstage to prepare for my performance (glugging away on a bottle of water as ever!), where I tried to focus on what I was about to do out there. It was the first time I'd got to sing a proper ballad on the show and it was an emotional song.

On stage everything just clicked, from the beautiful arrangement of the music to guitarist Adam Goldsmith's expert playing perched on a stool just behind me. When I finished everyone went mad – all the coaches were on their feet and so were the audience, which was just incredible. Danny had a big smile on his face and revealed I'd made all the hairs on his head and body stand on end, while Will said that calling my performance dope once wouldn't be enough, so he started saying 'dope' over and over again like a machine gun which was really funny. A smiley Tom said he'd known I had the power from day one, but now I was baring my soul he was enjoying my performances even more.

I felt so happy with what I'd done and the response I'd got, but as I stood there with Holly the emotion of having just sung that song hit me like a slap in the face. As the positive vibes from everyone flooded all over me my legs felt like they were about to buckle. The realisation came at me all at once – this was the end. But at the same time I was doing my best not to cry because I wanted to try and take it all in for the very last time.

By the time we recorded the results show I'd calmed down and was excited to perform for the final time alongside all the other semi-finalists on (appropriately enough!) 'You're The Voice' by John Farnham. It was surreal that we were doing that song because I'd written a whole arrangement for it at Potters a few years earlier, so I felt totally at home and as we strutted around the stage in pairs I think we all enjoyed letting our hair down.

Then all too quickly it was time for that horrible bit again, the results of the public vote. For my team's one and only place in the final it was between Ruth and me. Standing at the side of the stage together waiting to go on, she was looking a bit downhearted. 'Are you OK?' I asked. 'You've got nothing to worry about, you've got this in the bag.' She looked uncertain and replied: 'I don't know now...' I remember thinking that was a strange reply, but surely there was no way she wasn't getting to the final. I was 99 per cent sure of that, but there was still a tiny 1 per cent of me thinking, 'What if...?'

Waiting on the set for the all-important result to be revealed, the overriding thought going through my head was: 'Bye bye, Leanne.' So when Holly suddenly announced I was through to the final I was utterly gobsmacked. How the hell had that happened? This was insane! But while I was chuffed to bits, my first instinct was to reach out for Ruth and give her a big hug, because regardless of whether she'd thought she was going through or not, there'd been this expectation surrounding her and I didn't want her to be upset. 'Ruth, don't worry about this,' I whispered. 'You're gonna be a huge star anyway, I'm sure of it.'

I think everyone else was just as shocked as I was. None of us had been expecting this and when Jaz Ellington didn't get through either I think it kind of threw us all. No one had predicted this! All of us contestants thought we'd known who the finalists were going to be from the start, but now everything had been tipped on its head and the public had just voted the two favourites out of the competition. Suddenly there was everything to play for.

Chapter 9

The Final Countdown

There was no time to stand still and absorb the bombshell of the semi-final result or celebrate it in any way. Before the shock events had even registered, I had to shake myself down and get my head around the next stage. First thing the next morning we began rehearsing for the final. The final? I could barely believe it when I said those words to myself. It felt so bizarre to still be in the competition because mentally I had said goodbye to the show the day before. And yet here I was preparing to sing again in front of the nation.

The only downside was my voice was definitely getting tired. The best way to describe it is to say it feels like you've had a night out during which you've got drunk and smoked loads, and then the next morning you go to speak and there's nothing there. Well, that's what my voice was like when I emerged bright and early for a long day of rehearsals the morning after the semis, so I had to be really careful. And to top it off my general tiredness was now also manifesting itself in a 'watery eye', which just wouldn't stop all day, all week in fact. Not a great look when you're trying to keep your make-up intact for filming!

With the vocal fatigue to deal with, I was so lucky to have someone like Yvie Burnett on my side. She'd been my mentor throughout and there's no other word for it – she was brilliant. She'd listen to me worrying and panicking, then ask me to sing a little and calmly say, 'Well, it's all there, you just need to warm it up and do a few vocal exercises.' Hers was the voice of reason and just what I needed to hear to keep me calm before the final.

I decided to sing 'It's A Man's Man's Man's World' even though I'd never sung it before. I'd heard it on the radio a few times and always thought, 'Wow, that is some song!' I think the reason it came back to me now was because it conveyed a message I had wanted to get across all along, and I saw this as my chance. I didn't want the coaches, the audience, the people at home, or anybody really, to think I was just this scared little mouse that couldn't really perform and could only do sad songs, because that's not me at all.

'A Man's World' was still an emotional song, but took me in a totally different direction from the sadness of 'Run

To You'. It had attitude, anger, sass and power in its tone and its lyrics. I wanted people to see I also had all these attributes, that I had guts and was more than capable of singing a song that had balls. It was a perfect choice.

Rehearsals began for what was going to be the biggest show of them all and we had some of the longest days we'd ever experienced. We were starting around seven in the morning and working flat out for at least fourteen hours. The only plus side to the late finishes was, if you finished after eight in the evening, you were allowed to have a car to take you home. Before eight, you had to get a bus from Elstree back to the flat in Barnet, which would take at least an hour and when you're totally knackered that's the last thing you want to do!

It was also difficult once the show was on air because people began to recognise us, especially earlier on if I was sat with Sam Buttery, who stands out a mile with his big glasses and black quiff! You could feel all the passengers craning their necks to get a good look. Of course, the schoolkids wouldn't just look; they'd be over like a shot, swarming everywhere, firing questions. We didn't mind though and their enthusiasm for the show was really uplifting.

In the end I started getting taxis back instead of the bus on those days we finished early, but it wasn't because of the attention; I'd discovered some poor person had got stabbed with a screwdriver in the street just yards from where we were staying, so I decided paying a tenner for a cab was money well spent!

I could never quite get my head around being recognised. When I'd get tweeted saying, 'Did I just see @leannemitch walking out of Sainsbury's on Barnet High Street?', it was as if they were spotting someone else. If I walked down the street I'd be aware of people pointing and staring but I remained in this bubble where I almost convinced myself it wasn't me they were talking about. I couldn't quite take in the enormity of the show and the extent of people's reactions. It just felt so unreal.

One of the brilliant things about the show was how lovely the other coaches were to us. Danny would often be at the bar after the live shows, so he would always come over and chat and give me some advice. I introduced him to my brother Daniel one night who was totally beside himself and thought Danny was a top bloke – he put a picture of the two of them on Facebook straight away, obviously!

Will.i.am was always so nice to me, even though I was very much in awe of him. He's a man who started from nothing and has achieved so much. He came up to me in Elstree and we did that little banging of fists thing, and I was like, 'Whoa, I am so cool right this second!' He often used to pat his throat when he saw me and say, 'Just you look after this.' That was a lovely compliment, especially when my voice was hurting.

On the day of the semi-final Jessie J had asked us to go to her dressing room one by one, and we were speechless when she gave each of us a gift bag. In it was a pair of Beats by Dr Dre headphones, a Moleskine notebook and a fancy Lamy pen, with a greetings card that read: 'Leanne – wow! Run to your dreams, love Jessie J x.' I was really touched that she'd bother to do something like that and that she'd taken the time out to do so. That is impressively thoughtful.

She's also incredibly down to earth. When I went into her dressing room that time she looked a vision of beauty in this bonkers shiny purple catsuit. She looked amazing but you could see she wasn't quite sure and asked, 'Does this look all right? I can't tell. I want you to be honest – does it look all right or do I look like an idiot?' All I could say was, 'If I looked like you I'd wear it!'

One of the first things that hit me when I got through to the final was the realisation that I was going to get to sing on stage with Tom Jones! I mean, how amazing is that? This has to be every singer's dream.

We went for 'Mama Told Me Not To Come', because I really love that song and I thought it'd be a really cool one to do with him. It wasn't a big dramatic ballad for once, it was upbeat and a bit rocky and I knew we could have some fun with it. Tom and his management team decided my other solo effort was going to be 'Run To You'

– it had got such a big reaction the previous week so we thought we might as well do it again. But ever the wannabe perfectionist, I was determined to play with it a bit and try and push myself further with the arrangement.

Tom and I had the chance to spend much more time together that week and I was so excited when he revealed he was taking me to Ronnie Scott's (the legendary Soho jazz club) to rehearse one afternoon. I'd never been before but was aware of its immense reputation. Everyone has played there from Nina Simone to Jamie Cullum, and when I mentioned I was going to Tyler James – one of the other four finalists – he told me that Amy Winehouse, who'd been his best friend, had also played there and loved it.

We had the place to ourselves and when we got inside it was actually much smaller than I'd imagined, but the atmosphere was so brilliantly old school and cool and I just wanted to soak it all up. So many amazing people that I look up to have sung there and ever since that trip I have become a little bit obsessed with the place – I would love to sing there properly one day!

Those days running up to the final felt very weird without everyone else. There were only the four of us left – me for Team Tom, Vince Kidd for Team Jessie, Bo Bruce for Team Danny and for Team will.i.am it was Tyler James. There had been so many of us at the start and now everywhere seemed a bit empty and echoey. But having said that, the four of us had so much fun that week. It was a very special time and there was a real sense of camaraderie between us, which I appreciated and enjoyed.

One of the funniest days was when we had to film this trailer to publicise the grand finale. It was themed around the idea of the 'Fantastic Four Finalists' and we all had to pretend we were some kind of super-hero. I stood there with my hands on my hips like Wonder Woman and was described as 'the one with lungs that punch like missiles'. Bo did some karate-style hand actions and Tyler punched his fist out towards the camera and looked really cool.

Vince decided that he was going to use the shirt he always had wrapped round his waist as a cape and then jump off a pile of boxes so they could get the action-hero style shot, but he managed to practically land on his head! Luckily he came up laughing and let me tell you, that was one of the funniest things I've ever seen – you've got to love his efforts. After all the pressure of the previous few weeks, it was good to have some time to let our hair down and oh my God, I've never laughed so much as on that day.

Saying that, I always felt the odd one out from the other three finalists, but not in a bad way. The three of them had been scouted and I hadn't; all three of them had management, whereas I didn't. They were all Londoners and I wasn't. They all had this 'Yeah, I'm cool' thing going on, and I certainly didn't! But they were all lovely and there was a sense that we were all really supporting each other. Nobody else could know how we were feeling except for us four because we were all in it together. We were four very different singers and only one of us could be crowned 'The Voice', but despite Yvie constantly saying to me, 'You really could win this now so we really need to get this right!', I never once saw myself as a potential winner.

That said, I couldn't work out which of the others would win it either. One minute I'd think Bo, then I thought Tyler and then I'd change my mind and decide it'd be Vince. They were all so unique and all such good singers so I had no idea who the public would go for. But despite my fixed conviction it wouldn't be me, Yvie was determined to give me the best shot possible and pushed me constantly, determined to make me sing as well as I possibly could.

On the night before the final we did a live link-up to Chris Evans and Alex Jones on *The One Show*. We were all so exhausted and we'd all had a long day, plus we had no idea whether we were live or not and we couldn't even properly hear what was going on through our ear-pieces. I stood next to Tom while we tried to answer their questions and I remember Jessie J just mouthing 'I want to go home', which made us all laugh. I think we all needed to go home and get our energy levels up to cope with everything that was coming our way the next day.

The final was going to be one hell of a show and I was excited and determined to enjoy it because I had already got further than I'd ever expected. I really didn't have anything to lose – getting to the final was a big enough prize for me.

Excited as I was, my voice was still knackered and feeling the strain after six weeks of singing non-stop. So far it felt like I'd been running off pure adrenaline and I wasn't sure what was left in me at this point, whether I had any more reserves of energy I could draw on. However, in rehearsal as I listened to the arrangement with the band for 'A Man's World', I could hear it sounded amazing – it was dramatic, full of attitude and I couldn't wait to get out there that evening and perform it.

Of course there were a few nerves, but no major butterflies and no rising panic because I didn't feel under any pressure. If I was going to be the first one out, to do so singing 'A Man's World' would be an incredible way to go. That evening as I stood there on stage, waiting in that split second for the music to start, I could feel the excitement fizzing from everyone and I just wanted to do this song justice and have the time of my life doing so.

I also realised I had something to prove with this number. I really wanted to show that I was a performer as well as a singer, and more importantly, because I'd beaten Ruth Brown to the final and so many people had wanted her to go through, I needed to prove my worth. This was the time to show everyone that I actually did deserve to be in the final four, even if I wasn't sure I believed it myself. I had to give this my all so I could be proud of this final performance. I truly believed that when they froze the voting phone-lines halfway through the show, my time would be up, so I needed to go out in style.

I loved singing that song and felt I'd really performed with attitude and had shown another side of me. I put in as many tricks as possible without making it sound too over the top and tried to show my sassy side. I felt I'd achieved what I wanted to and was happy to leave on my own personal high note ... quite literally!

When I looked up and saw all the coaches on their feet, the feeling was brilliant. It was an empowering moment to get a standing ovation in the final from four such talented people. Also the audience wouldn't stop cheering, which totally blew me away. You can see in my face how happy I am. I couldn't stop beaming.

Tom also had a big grin on his face and said some lovely things that I'll never forget. 'What you see is what you get with Leanne,' he began. 'She's a very natural person and she's the same off stage as she is on stage. And I think, and I hope, that's why people have warmed to her. And of course there's that fantastic voice!' which got another big cheer. I was staggered by the praise from all the coaches. I couldn't have asked for nicer feedback and I felt truly humbled to be standing on that stage in front of them.

Next came my duet with Tom. This really was my 'pinch me, I must be dreaming' moment. I knew being on stage with Sir Tom Jones singing one of his classics was something I was going to cherish for the rest of my life, but in the meantime I had to concentrate on what we were doing. I needed to be able to perform with conviction and not just stand there mouthing, 'Oh my God, look, everybody – I'm singing with Tom Jones!' Not that it was easy! He had this really cheeky glint in his eye and a smile of enjoyment on his face. But we rocked it and now it's wicked to be able to say I've done it. What an absolute pleasure and one to tick off my bucket list!

I knew it would be fun because all the rehearsals for that song had been so entertaining. Each time we rehearsed he did it a different way so every time I was trying to follow him. With Tom, he's a tremendous force of skill and spirit. There was no point giving him a lyric sheet with direct instructions on what to sing and where to sing it, because he'd pay no attention. He just did what felt right, with incredible results, and not only did I love it, I knew I could learn from it.

After the duet, the voting was frozen and when the result was in the shockwaves reverberated around the studio. No one could believe it: Vince was gone! I was thrown into a state of confusion about what the hell was going on. This was ridiculous, totally crazy and not how things were supposed to be. I don't know what freaked me out more – me still being there or Vince having gone. Somehow I'd made it into the final three!

The shock kept echoing around in my head. Now it was just between Bo, Tyler and me, and at this point I did start to think, even if this is a fluke, I'm still here and it really could be any one of us. I had no idea how people were voting – I couldn't predict this any more. I just couldn't get my head around it, so I knew I had to stop trying. I focused on having another chance to show even more of what I could do. I was like, 'I really have nothing to lose now, apart from my sanity!'

Because it's a live show, all these thoughts were flying through my head at breakneck speed. As soon as the vote had come through, I was yanked off stage, had to run (and I mean literally run!) behind the audience and out the stage door, and then leg it up the corridor to where I had to do a quick wardrobe change, plus make-up and hair at 100 miles per hour. Everywhere I looked people were chasing me, calling me, literally pushing me from one place to the other, like get in here, get in there, doing my hair, doing my face, pulling this up, pulling that in and zipping me up.

I was surrounded by people sewing me in something, sewing some decoration on to me, and sewing my top to the bra strap so it didn't fall down and I was trying to stay calm and focused at the centre of all this whirlwind of activity.

It's so quick you don't have time to breathe and in those situations you just have to surrender all sense of dignity and accept the grabbing and shoving because you know time is of the essence. There's no time to object or worry about 'personal space' issues even if you wanted to!

One thing that had been troubling me that day was I still had this watery eye. It had been doing it all week, but now it had stepped up a notch. It didn't stop for the whole day so the make-up team had done my whole face except for this one eye. Even twenty minutes before we went live, it was still watering away. The production team were yelling that they needed me on stage NOW and the make-up girls were shouting back 'She's not done yet!' as they tried ever so carefully to stick a false eyelash to this squinty eye and re-touch my make-up.

The make-up girls did a great job and were very reassuring to have around, because it could have been a nightmare. I was like, 'Of all the things that I don't need to be worrying about right now, top of the list is a flippin' watery eye!' It was as if someone somewhere had decreed: 'We're not going to make this easy for you today. We won't be so cruel as to take away your voice, we'll let you get through it that way, but you're only going to do it with one eye slowly running down your face...'

Taking to the stage for the third time that evening to sing 'Run To You' was nerve-wracking. I had entered *The Voice*

because I wanted to push myself and see where I could get
– I never thought I would get anywhere near the final. Yet
here I was! All at once the enormity of the situation I found
myself in hit me and I knew this had to be the performance
of my life. It may sound melodramatic but suddenly I knew
what the phrase 'singing for your life' really meant.

It wasn't that I couldn't mess up, or I had to give it my all
– I'd been doing that all along. I just had to find something
extra deep inside me to make this performance beyond
extraordinary. My thoughts turned to the many people
who had been rooting for me, those who had felt strongly
enough to vote for me, everyone that had sent me such
lovely messages on Twitter and of course my family.

They'd got me through to this final, and I was doing this
for all of them to show them how grateful I was to be there.
I was going to give it my all and in doing so I hoped to
be able to give back to Rob, my parents, my friends and
everyone that had supported me. These thoughts came with
me on stage and stayed with me through every moment of
the song, and before I knew it I was softly singing the last
line of my last ever performance on *The Voice*.

Suddenly the audience went wild and at that moment I
could feel myself letting go of my emotions. Holly came
over and put her arm around me and I could feel the
warmth from everyone, the coaches and all the people in
the audience. I could see some of them were crying, and

others had tears in their eyes. I was overwhelmed by the strength of emotion all around me. Maybe it was because no one had really expected me to get this far, maybe it was the song, I don't know, but by the time I'd got more lovely feedback from the coaches I just felt an emotional wreck.

Then before we knew it the momentous moment of truth had arrived. This was it. No running for the hills now – Holly Willoughby was about to announce the first ever winner of *The Voice UK*. And I never in my wildest dreams expected her to say what she did next...

Chapter 10

Beyond *The Voice*

I still find it so weird and a little unbelievable that complete strangers voted for me. I know my friends and family did, obviously, and everyone from Potters and even people probably from my area, but it's so hard to get your head around the fact that people who don't know you are also rooting and voting for you. It kind of blows my mind and I am so grateful – winning *The Voice* has given me opportunities I could only have dreamed about a year ago.

I managed to get in a few days abroad with my family not long after the final, and even there I had loads of kids coming up to me asking for autographs and photos, going, 'I voted for you!', or their parents saying, 'Oh God, she loves you, she absolutely loves you.' I just didn't expect that at all, especially from kids. I thought I knew what type of people and age range I would appeal to, so it really does take me by surprise that I have fans who are kids and teenagers too.

Amongst all the excitement and anticipation for what the future holds, it feels very odd and a little sad to have left the place where I have worked and been so happy for so many years. Everyone at Potters was massively supportive of me during my time on *The Voice*; they even played the final live on a huge screen in the main theatre and postponed that evening's show just so everyone could watch it and enjoy the moment with me. It really does get me to think I honestly thought I knew where my life was heading (or staying rather!) and now it's taking such a completely different path. I couldn't in a million years have expected something as life-changing as this to happen to me.

The first couple of weeks after the final were a complete and utter whirlwind. There's no other way to describe it. The morning after winning I had to pack up the flat in Barnet I'd been staying in for the past eight weeks – it was now crammed with all my rubbish which my parents had to take home. Then on the same day I had to do God knows how many phone interviews as well as travel to Manchester to do *BBC Breakfast* the following morning. I watched that interview back before writing this, and I can see how much I hadn't got a bloody clue what was going on or what I was doing. I was knackered and a bit dazed!

I must have done about twenty radio interviews that day,

some magazine chats and more TV before I travelled back to London that evening. This newspaper, magazine, telly and radio interview process then filled every day for the rest of that week... It was such a bonkers time, but I met some really lovely people and they all seemed so happy for me, which was brilliant.

There was only one thing I didn't enjoy as much during that time, which was shooting a video for 'Run To You'. I suppose I was still in a state of shock about winning, but I didn't realise 'Run To You, was being released as a single and didn't understand why we were making a video for it so long after the event. With it being the BBC, they obviously can't advertise the fact that they've put your single on i-tunes. As a result no one really knew the single was available, so I was surprised they wanted to go to the trouble of making a music video for it.

I'd never done anything like this before and I didn't really know what to do. On the day of the shoot I turned up presuming they'd watched me on the show, seen how I like to look and would be able to recreate it for the shoot. It turned out that wasn't the case. They were different hair and make-up stylists to the people I was used to on the show, and although it started off OK for the first 'look', I didn't like how I looked for the rest of the video.

The timescale is very short on a video shoot, which I have now realised is normal for these things, so to get everything done (in one day) the stylists have to be very quick in between shots. This resulted in my hair not looking its best, in my opinion! There's one shot where my hair is just up in some sort of knot with my fringe pulled back. The hair guy, as nice as he was, when I questioned the style, just went, 'Oh, it looks fine.' That's not exactly confidence boosting! My hair is a massive part of my image and when you're performing you need to feel good about yourself. I like my hair big, not scraped back as I'd have it if I were cleaning the house or something!

I also wear massive eyelashes but they only had these tiny little things, and I wasn't very keen on the clothes either. No one had actually bothered to ask me, 'What do you want to wear?' I kind of felt the same as on that first live show of *The Voice* – I just didn't feel like me. When I watched the finished edit back I didn't know what to think, but I knew I was at the beginning of a huge learning curve. This was my first ever video; it wasn't going to be perfect.

The director guy told me how to mime to the music, saying I shouldn't open my mouth too wide and that I should just speak the lyrics as they played it back. They didn't want me to sing along properly because they actually play the music back to you at around thirty times faster than the original speed, then they slow it down in the edit in order to capture some of the special effects happening around you. I said, 'But I'm hardly moving my mouth when I'm singing!' I didn't feel comfortable with it as it was so unlike anything I'd done before but everyone reassured me: 'Don't worry, it will look really good.'

Well, to my eyes it doesn't look natural at all. My mouth is moving out of sync with the music and it looks like I'm barely even miming or that I'm miming along to another song completely. Watching it back now it makes me laugh and cringe a bit at the same time – I guess that's another lesson learned then, Leanne! In future, I need to get much more involved in the creative process and I'll always trust my own instincts. You know yourself better than anyone else ever will, so don't let anybody try and change you if you don't want to be changed.

At that point, I'll admit that I felt pretty lost. I hadn't chosen a manager at this point so I wasn't sure who to turn to for guidance, to talk things through in these new situations and in this intimidating and fast-moving new world.

One of the really positive things about *The Voice* is the fact that you're not signing your life away when you win. You have got the power to do what you want up to a point after the show has ended, and you know you have got some say in your future career. However, at the same time you need someone looking after you as well.

I really wanted to be excited about what was happening; this was what I'd worked all my life for and I couldn't believe it was happening to me. But it took a while for things to gradually calm down and let me see the wood through the trees, so to speak! When I finally had time to appoint a manager and Colin Lester at Twenty First Artists was on board, everything began to fall into place. As soon as I started work on my proper debut album I felt like the luckiest person on the planet – this was something I'd genuinely always dreamt about and here it was, finally coming true.

Although the thought of writing it was daunting, I was really looking forward to making something of which I could be proud. I couldn't stop grinning to myself every time I remembered it was actually happening!

I was told I would be making the album with Brian Rawling at Metrophonic Music. Brian is a Grammy award-winning producer and has worked with everyone from Cher and Kylie Minogue to David Bowie and Girls Aloud. So this was certainly a step up from the last 'studio' I recorded an album in, back in Suffolk! Brian's team are based in a big house set in the countryside on the outskirts of London, which has lots of outbuildings that have been converted into studios. It's a great place to work and as soon as you enter it immediately feels like a really creative and productive environment to be in. Needless to say, I was totally in my element.

The first week I was there a big red Ferrari was on the gravel driveway and I found out it was on loan to one of the JLS boys, who was trying it out for size. They were working on their new album and were all sat around one of the tables having their lunch one day, and as I walked in, I thought, 'Hmmm, shall I go and sit with them or just find a corner to hide in?' I opted for the corner. This new world I was in was taking some getting used to, and I was nowhere near accustomed to it yet.

Brian and his team are without doubt amongst the best in the business, and when he asked me what type of album I wanted to do, I knew I wanted to write a lot of it. However, I was also honest with him and said although I wasn't sure exactly what direction I wanted to go in, there was no way I was going to make a covers album.

He asked me about my background and I explained I'd always written my own songs and how important this was to me. I also admitted that if we were to do my own songs, I really would want to take as much time as possible to get it right. I think past experiences had made me a little wary, and this time I wanted to know I was going to be happy with anything that was produced.

He then asked to hear some of my stuff. I was terrified: here I was letting some of the top names in the business listen to my music, which had been home-recorded through my crappy little mixing desk and my old electric organ, which I've now had for about eighteen years! As they listened along, the first thing they asked was, 'Who did you write these with?' I said I'd written them myself. They looked at me and said, 'Yes, but who do you write with?' I had to explain I don't work with anyone. I only do it for fun so I just write completely on my own. They explained these days they usually write in teams, so I guess that's why the prospect of writing solely for fun didn't initially register with them!

Writing with other people was not something I'd ever done before, so I couldn't quite imagine how this arrangement would work. The first songwriter I met was a guy called Paul Barry and as I looked around his writing studio, I was greeted by the sight of dozens and dozens of gleaming platinum albums covering the walls.

He's a three-time Ivor Novello award winner and has written some of the biggest songs ever including Cher's 'Believe' and 'Hero' by Enrique Iglesias. He has also worked with the likes of Britney Spears and Celine Dion. And now he was here with Lowestoft's finest – me! As you can imagine, it was a tad intimidating meeting and writing with him at first, but he was a lovely guy and was able to put me at my ease from the off. I soon found I was loving it. Here I was being given the chance to talk, live and breathe music all day. Life didn't get much better than this – to me this lifestyle was just brilliant.

Over the next week or so, I wrote with lots of different writers to see what worked and what didn't so much. It was a fantastic process. All the writers I met were so talented, and it soon became apparent which ones I clicked with best.

For me, the way I'd written in the past had always been solitary, and as I'd only ever written as a hobby for myself and not for performance, I'd write about what I was thinking at the time, or to express something that had been troubling me. Now having met some really good writing partners, I was working in a slightly different way and I loved it. I was still drawing on my own experiences in life, but I was shaping the lyrics with the help of someone else, so they now had another perspective and slant to them as well.

The first song we wrote was actually called 'Between The Devil And The Deep Blue Sea' and it's about feeling like you're suffocating. It describes that sensation when everything's becoming too much, when there's too much pressure and you want to run for the hills. But at the same time you want to stay where you are, doing what you're doing, because even though you are out of your depth, you know you love it and that sometimes you have to step outside of your comfort zone. I think everyone will be able to guess what that one's about!

So songs can come from anywhere and on the album there's plenty about how I'm feeling. Some are more obvious than others, but a lot could mean one thing to me and something totally different to the person that's listening to it. Which is what I really like about them. Each day would start with, 'So what do you wanna write today?' I'd think, 'How am I feeling? Happy? Grumpy? OK, let's write about that then.' Or the spark could be thinking about something that has happened in the past. Sometimes I use other people as inspiration, if I've been thinking about someone close to me and dwelling on something they're going through. I can imagine how they must be feeling and channel those emotions in my song.

Anyway, it's a starting point and it's amazing how much can tumble out from just asking yourself a simple question. Events you thought long forgotten are clearly recalled and you remember exactly the emotions they evoked at the time, whatever they may be. Suddenly you have something forming and everyone in the room gets it and is behind it, which makes it a totally exhilarating process. I love being at the centre of that.

When it starts to sound like an actual song and your vocals have been properly mixed and produced, it suddenly takes on a whole new life of its own. You listen and you can imagine it playing on the radio or in someone's house and you hear it how other people might hear it, and at that point you can actually feel a little bit proud. That is the most brilliant and satisfying feeling in the world. It's also so intoxicating when you see other people at the studio – the other writers, the mixers, the musicians – getting excited about it as well.

I was surprised at how quickly we could write the songs, yet I was so pleased with all of them. As well as the ones

I'd done with a partner, there are songs I've written on my own, and every single song on the album is drawn from my personal experiences.

There's another track we recorded called 'Walk You Home', which I love because it's quite an introspective song for me. It's quieter, quite wistful and there's just a cello playing in the background; it's not all about the big vocal.

It was one of the longest days we'd had in the studio and everyone was knackered – earlier that day I'd put down the vocals for three other songs. Maybe because we'd just done a dramatic big vocal number we all wanted to mellow out a bit – so we started playing around with some chords when we suddenly realised we were onto something. It's funny because when that magic happens you do start to get really excited – you're all on the same page thinking: 'Yeah, this is wicked – this is gonna be really good!' It's such an adrenaline rush!

We must've been there until the early hours of the morning writing 'Walk You Home', but in a situation like that you don't care about the time. You don't care that you're knackered, or that you've had a long day, because you're doing something you love and that's what it's all about for me.

Lyrically the song can mean different things to different people, whether it's about someone close to you passing away or someone going through a tough time and you're trying to help them. As I said before, when I write lyrics they have to mean something to me and I was thinking about a few different things when I wrote this one.

A while ago I'd had a heated conversation with someone, but hadn't been aware of the stress they were going through at the time as I was too caught up in my own stuff. That was partly the inspiration, as was the death of my lovely Grandad Bert four years ago. I know how sad I felt at the time, but for my mum it was much worse. So I suppose the song is about looking out for someone else, being strong for other people around you and forgetting about your own crap for a while.

I wrote what would become my debut single, 'If I Knew Then', with two of the songwriting team at Metrophonic, Ben Adams and Lee McCutcheon. We'd written a couple of songs together for the album already and seemed to click well. When you're writing, you can sometimes sit there for hours and feel like all you have in your head is a brick wall. Then other times you can have a song written and recorded within 2 hours – 'If I Knew Then' was one of those.

As soon as we started playing around with chords, we felt it had this great soulful feel about it. It's a great feeling when you just start scribbling on a piece of paper and it flows out of you. I guess the song is a lot about a feeling of regret. Or maybe, not regret, but thinking about if you'd have done something differently, would it have changed the way you are today? I, personally, don't like to have regrets, I believe everything happens for a reason and sometimes you have to leave it to fate. But I do have a past, like everyone else, and naturally, like everyone, always wonder *what if*? I'm really proud of this song, I feel like it epitomizes who I am as a singer. Yes, it is an emotional ballad, but I think, with a bit of kick!

I'm really proud of the whole album and wanted to give it my all. There's a lot of hard work that has gone into it and that's why I'm so glad other people are loving it too. I have been getting tweets from everywhere from France to Brazil about it, which is so exciting and such a relief. After I won *The Voice* all I wanted to do was to take my time and make the best album I could. I didn't want to rush into anything – I had been given the most amazing opportunity and I was determined to enjoy every last bit of it.

I did a couple of recordings at the Sphere Studios in Battersea, south London, and after my session I was taken into the main studio there. It was massive and could fit a whole orchestra inside it. As I was given the guided tour I was told this was the room where Tom had recorded the Bond title-track 'Thunderball' and had famously fainted in the vocal booth as he held on to that final mega-high note!

The first time I heard my album all the way through was such a surreal moment. I tried to concentrate fully but I kept thinking, how the hell did this all happen within the space of a matter of months? So much had just happened, and yet this time last year I'd got married, I was working in Potters and genuinely content in my happy, normal and quite average life. Since then I'd been on national TV, sung with Sir Tom Jones, won *The Voice* and now, with the help of Britain's top musical talent, I had just cut my own album. Unbelievable and unreal – these words barely began to describe the situation I now found myself in.

Just when I thought things couldn't get any more surreal I ended up meeting Prince Harry at an awards ceremony at the seriously posh Intercontinental Hotel on Park Lane in London. It was in aid of the WellChild charity and is a fantastic event that celebrates the bravery of some of the country's seriously ill children and the dedication of those who care for them, and can really make a difference to their lives.

It was such a humbling experience to meet these amazing kids. That night also marked the first live singing performance I'd agreed to since *The Voice* and it felt great to be performing again. I'd been holed up in the recording studio for months, probably the longest I'd ever gone without singing in public, and I was so nervous! But what an amazing first gig to do, and truly special.

Meeting Prince Harry was just one of the most random moments of my life. We had to line up to be introduced to him and it turned out he was a fan of *The Voice* and we chatted away about that for a while because he wanted to know what life had really been like on Team Tom. He said I looked different in real life to how I'd looked on the telly. 'Is that a good thing or a bad thing?' I replied, giggling nervously. It all seemed so bizarre because I never thought someone like me would ever meet an actual prince, but he was a lovely guy and I was so impressed with how much time he spent with the children and how natural he was with them.

I'd caught up with Tom a few months after *The Voice* when he played at Newmarket Races. I knew a week before he'd had to cancel a couple of dates because he'd got bronchitis. But as I watched him from the VIP area performing for two hours without stopping, he was an amazing force of energy and charisma. There wasn't a hint of illness about him. The audience went crazy for him and there couldn't have been a single person there who wasn't in awe of this man. His voice is incredible and I don't think there is anybody that's coming up in the ranks who will be anything like him. He is totally unique.

I'd brought along my friends Mel, Caroline and Kizzy that night. They had dropped everything to come when I told them there was a chance we might meet Tom at some point during the evening – they were practically racing out the door the minute I asked them!

We met up with Tom before he was due to go on stage and

my friend Kizzy, who is admittedly a bit of a ditz, thought she had to curtsey because he's a Sir. He was so relaxed and welcoming to all of them and I could see, one by one, they had fallen under his spell and were completely in love with him. As they reluctantly said goodbye, Kizzy did her little half curtsey, which was hilarious!

I then had a really good chat with him and he was full of questions about the album, the songs and the team, and asking how I was enjoying the process. It was like talking to a good friend and he was as positive and as encouraging as ever.

Watching him backstage that night or when I've been with him in the street, he's always been an absolute gentleman when it comes to signing autographs or having a quick chat with his fans. He's a natural at it, whereas it's still taking some time for me to get used to it.

After spending the rest of 2012 in the studio, the new year brought along some more new experiences, the National Television Awards being one of them. This was also going to be my first time walking down the infamous 'red carpet'. Now, I'm first and foremost a singer. So the thought of having to walk down and stand on a red carpet with people looking at me from all angles scared me to death! As I pulled up to the sea of flashing cameras, I felt sick.

I got out of the car, and the only way I can describe it is mental! The noise of people shouting and calling out names was unreal and there I was stood next to Torvill and Dean, Keith Lemon, half of *Coronation Street* and Holly Willoughby! This was another 'am I supposed to be here?' moment. I spoke to journalists from Radio 1, *This Morning*, Heart FM and loads of big online sites. It felt great – mainly because it was the first time I was able to tell everyone what I'd been up to since *The Voice* and what was coming up, and that I hadn't disappeared off the planet!

After that I did the 'stand there and smile' photos in front of the paps before finally being allowed in for the awards. It turned out to be a really nice night and it was good to catch up with Holly and Reggie and some of the guys from the show.

I've never sung for the fame; the only reason I went in for the show in the first place was because it was all about the voice and not about being a celebrity. I still live in normal Lowestoft and can't imagine being anywhere else. I just do not know how to be a 'celebrity'. There is no handbook, no set rules; I can't work at it like I do my songwriting. For someone like Tom, there is a magic about him that makes it look so easy.

I think maybe that's why I found it so hard that first week of being chucked into this fame game when the show finished. Outside *BBC Breakfast* in Manchester that first morning were a load of paparazzi and I hated it. Did they want me to wave? Did they want me to fall over? I had no idea why they were there. It certainly wasn't about the music and I was really uncomfortable with it. For me that kind of thing is the downside of fame, but when it comes to the positives the good outweighs the bad and I've just got to learn to deal with it.

If anybody ever writes or says any crap about me online or in the media, you can't take it to heart and ignoring it is the only way to cope. It's the same as it was with those bitchy comments I got from a few schoolmates back when I was a teenager – you just have to develop a thick skin. I now understand that comes with the job and you just have to remember that these people don't know you at all. Luckily I have my family and my friends who love me for me and not for what others think of me.

One question I keep being asked when people tweet me or when I meet them in the street is if I'd recommend them going on the show. To which I'd have to say only enter it if you're entering it for the right reason, which is hopefully because you love singing. If not then go and do another show. *The Voice* is what it says on the tin – they want you to sing and anything else is secondary.

People also want tips for that first *Voice* audition. I can't say don't be nervous because I was terrified. I can't really say be confident, because I wasn't at all. The only advice I can give is: be prepared with what you're singing and know how you're going to sing it. Oh, and if you want to do it how I did it, drink plenty of water!

The other day someone asked me what I'd learned about myself during this whole crazy experience. I've learned so much, but I think one of the most important lessons is that I can push myself even more than I thought, and not just vocally. I've also learned I can actually take a lot more than I thought I could, pressure-wise, and I'm quite good at handling difficult or stressful situations (apart from the 'Pink' week!). This was an aspect of myself that surprised me while we were filming the show.

I've always been the person that would help someone else who's in need of calming down or whatever, but it's important to remember ultimately we're only singing – it's not like we're on the front line of a war or anything. When you remind yourself of that you gain a perspective, which keeps you sane.

Also I have learned that if you want to stay true to yourself, then it means speaking up when you don't want to do something. It's a lesson I have maybe yet to completely master, as the 'Run To You' video proved! But now I know next time I need to make sure my input is valued and things do not run out of my control so much. I have the right to have a say about things creatively and to be listened to and now I'll always only do things I'm proud to do. So I suppose you could say this process really has helped me find my voice in more ways than one.

Otherwise I don't think I've changed much as a person

since I was that teenager who turned down a recording contract aged fourteen. Like everyone over time, I have become a bit more grown up, and I can handle things a little bit more now. So much of that is because I'm lucky enough to be pretty stable and have a support network around me. Having the strength of those around me to lean on when things are rough has helped keep me strong.

I couldn't have got to this point without any of them and I felt so happy that I could let them be the first to hear what I'd been up to in the studio. I hope they are proud of me because I sure as hell am so grateful to them.

Rob is now obsessed with the new songs. He has them in his car, listens to them all the time and I know he is happy for me and proud of me. There's a couple of songs that my mum admits she can't listen to without crying and she also revealed Dad got teary when she played him some of the album for the first time. To know that my music has touched the people I care about the most means the world to me.

I owe my parents so much. We weren't the most well off of families and yet they bought me my first PA, paid for my singing lessons, the organ lessons and the Dusmagrik theatre club. It must have cost them a fortune every week and I know for sure that if it hadn't been for them I probably wouldn't be doing this now.

It wasn't just the financial support though, of course.

If they hadn't been with me every step of the way, giving me a nudge when I needed one, I might have just stayed in my bedroom trilling away to 'Sailing' and never had the confidence to take things any further.

As for the future, it's a funny but exciting feeling not knowing what it holds.

I live for today, not tomorrow, and as ever I will always be a realist. I'll never let my head or my wildest dreams run away with me, and I'll always keep my feet firmly on the ground. I sing because I love it but I can't deny the unbelievable kick I get when I see that others are enjoying it too. I think if you love something you're doing and other people can feel it and can see how much you love it, then that's the best feeling in the world.

People ask me what I've learned... Well, I now know my parents taught me the most valuable lesson of all. That if you love something enough, and you are prepared to work hard at it, then it really can become your life...

Acknowledgements

I'd like to thank my Mum and Dad for taking me to all my singing/music/drama lessons night after night as a kid, and costing them a bucket load in the meantime! And my brother Daniel for putting up with it all!! My husband Rob for always being by my side. And my friend Melissa for never giving up on me! Also, my teachers for singing, organ and theatre school: Richard, Cathy and Dusty. I was very lucky to have them.

I'd like to thank everyone at *The Voice* for all their help and support, and giving me that life changing Blind Audition. Thank you to everyone at Decca Records. Thanks to Colin Lester, Alex Fisher and everyone at Twenty First Artists for their support and guidance. Finally, Sir Tom Jones, for believing in me and picking me!